SICILY
in your pocket

Travel Publications

MAIN CONTRIBUTOR: Russell Chamberlin

PHOTOGRAPH CREDITS
All photos supplied by The Travel Library:
Stuart Black front cover, back cover, title page, 7,
11, 12, 17, 21, 22, 26, 28(t), 36, 37(t), 38, 39, 43,
47(b), 48, 54, 55, 62, 65, 67, 69, 71, 79, 84, 86, 88,
91, 96, 104; Stephen Coyne 52, 53, 59, 121; Philip
Enticknap 46, 47(t), 50, 101; David Lyons 9, 14,
20, 28(b), 45, 56, 73, 93, 109, 113, 116, 122;
Antonio Noto 80, 81, 82, 83, 110; R Richardson 19,
24, 27, 30, 31, 35, 40, 85, 119, 125; Gino Russo 5,
18, 29, 32, 33, 37(b), 41, 60, 74, 77, 78, 87, 89, 92,
94, 107.

*Front cover: Cefalù beach; back cover: Temple of
Concord, Agrigento; title page: fishing boats in harbour,
Aspra, near Palermo.*

While every effort is made to ensure that the information in this guide is as accurate and up-to-date as
possible, detailed information is constantly changing. The publisher cannot accept responsibility for any
consequences resulting from changes in information, errors or omissions.

MANUFACTURE FRANÇAISE DES PNEUMATIQUES MICHELIN

Place des Carmes-Déchaux – 63000 Clermont-Ferrand (France)

© Michelin et Cie. Propriétaires-Éditeurs 1998

Dépôt légal Avril 98 – ISBN 2-06-652201-5 – ISSN 1272-1689

No part of this publication may be reproduced in any form

without the prior permission of the publisher.

Printed in Spain 11-00/4

MICHELIN TRAVEL PUBLICATIONS
Michelin Tyre plc
The Edward Hyde Building
38 Clarendon Road
WATFORD Herts WD1 1SX - UK
☎ (01923) 415000
www.michelin-travel.com

MICHELIN TRAVEL PUBLICATIONS
Michelin North America
One Parkway South
GREENVILLE, SC 29615
☎ 1-800 423-0485
www.michelin-travel.com

CONTENTS

INTRODUCTION

Sicily is Italy's largest island, indeed it is the largest in the Mediterranean. It is a land of contrasts, which may surprise the first-time visitor: with its dramatic volcanic mountains, and the blossom-covered almond and citrus groves which fill the valleys in spring. Time seems to have stood still in the remote hill-top villages of the interior, many with haunting ancient ruins, while the bustling coastal cities have all the attractions the modern tourist would expect. The supremely beautiful yet dramatic coastline has beaches backed by steeply rising mountains in the east, rocky coves, and fishing villages nestling on narrow coastal strips.

Colourful boats in the fashionable resort of Mondello, near Palermo.

The scenery and views are often breathtaking, especially during spring when the land is covered with flowers and blossom, but it is also a land steeped in history. The treasurehouse of monuments is testimony to the island's rich cultural heritage. Sicily's strategic position has meant that the island's destiny has been shaped by a series of invaders who have sought to dominate this triangle of land situated at the crossroads between Africa and the Mediterranean lands. The first to arrive were the Greeks, followed by the Carthaginians and Romans, the Vandals, Goths and Byzantines. The Normans introduced eclectic culture in the 11C, and over the next 700 years Germans, Spanish and French battled for possession of the island.

The result is a land rich in historic monuments and art treasures: few places can rival the Greek temples and Roman theatres of Syracuse, Agrigento, Segesta and magical Taormina; the charming medieval streets of Erice; the majestic Norman cathedrals of Monreale and Cefalù, with their stunning Byzantine mosaics – all contrasting with the growing coastal resorts on the north and east coasts. Of course, no visit is complete without exploring the vibrant street life of the island's capital, Palermo, now undergoing something of a revival with the restoration of its splendid medieval and Baroque monuments.

GEOGRAPHY

Sicily is the largest island in the Mediterranean Sea, with an area of 25 709km^2 (9 927sq miles) and a population of around 5 million people. Its name in antiquity, *Trinacria* (three-cornered), describes its curiously regular triangular shape. It is separated from the mainland by the Strait of Messina, 3km (2 miles) wide at their narrowest point, with a railway ferry running between Messina and Reggio di Calabria.

The north and east coasts are mountainous, with a particularly dramatic range behind the capital, Palermo. Here the mountains come close to the sea, leaving only a narrow coastal strip for the railway and coast road.

The interior and south are mostly undulating country except for the extraordinary bluff, 1 000m (3 289ft) high, on which the city of Enna is built. A railway runs along the northern and eastern coasts, and cross-country from Catania to Agrigento. Until recently the interior was badly served by roads but there is now a system of motorways (*autostrade*) and the major roads have been upgraded with a spectacular range of viaducts along the south-western coast.

A Greek myth tells how a giant was pinned down under Sicily so that every time he moved, the island moved. The reason for the myth is very evident, for Sicily, with its two active volcanoes and frequent earthquakes, is geologically the most unstable of all European regions. The most violent recent earthquake was that of Messina in 1908 when some 80 000 people

The north coast of Sicily, looking east from the Roman remains at Solunto, with the craggy hills of the Madonie Mountains in the distance.

were killed, arousing the compassion of all Europe. The volcano Stromboli occupies an island all to itself, with a small town crouching at its feet. Etna, at 3 340m (10 958ft), dominates the eastern coast. Like Fujiyama in Japan, it is supremely elegant in shape: an almost perfect cone, capped with snow and with a white plume streaming from it like a heraldic banner. Its eruption in 1669 destroyed almost totally the great city of Catania at its feet, and those living in its vicinity have long since become accustomed to showers of ash and occasional stones.

One of the memorable impressions of Sicily in the spring is the vividness of its wild flowers. Agriculture is the major industry, with an emphasis on citrus fruits. The area around Catania, extending deep into the interior, is one vast orange grove, while orange trees are grown ornamentally in almost every town.

Emigration, particularly among the peasantry, has led to depopulation in many areas of the interior, while the development of tourism has led to considerable expansion of the coastal towns. It must be admitted that town planning has not been a Sicilian strength, and a considerable amount of unlovely sprawl, including many unfinished buildings, stretches deep into the countryside. However, the problem has now been recognised and the creation of a national park around Etna is an example of the measures being taken to remedy the situation.

HISTORY

The story of Sicily reflects the story of mankind in the Mediterranean, from the first evidence of the human ability to think, to the current problems of Europe. The oldest remains are the cave paintings in the Addaura Caves on Monte Pellegrino north of Palermo, reputed to be around 10 000 years old. There are remains of a prehistoric village at Punta Milazzese, on Panarea, one of the Lipari Islands.

Every subsequent period in human history has left its mark in some form, much of it finding expression in art, myth or legend. It was from the eastern shore that the Cyclops Polyphemus hurled vast rocks to

A prehistoric village at Punta Milazzese, on Panarea, one of the Lipari Islands.

sink the boat of Ulysses, and the Roman poet Virgil brought his hero, Aeneas. In Syracuse, you can still see the fountain the nymph Arethusa was turned into in order to escape the river-god Alpheus.

The Hellenic Invasions

About 700 BC Semitic Carthaginians from North Africa established colonies on Sicily, but it was the **Greeks**, those consummate sailors endlessly curious about the world around them, who brought civilisation to the island. Cautiously feeling their way westwards towards the Pillars of Hercules and the vast Atlantic Ocean beyond, they encountered the island. Some continued north, braving the terrors of the monsters Scylla and Charybdis (whirlpools and rocks in the Strait of Messina), to the coast of mainland Italy where they settled, but most were content to settle on the amazingly fertile eastern and southern coasts of the island, gradually spreading out all around the coast. The Greek remains on Sicily today probably outclass in quantity, if not in quality, the remains on mainland Greece.

The Greeks brought civilisation but certainly not peace, importing instead the jealousies and hatreds between cities that were part of Greek mainland culture. The city of Corinth, deadly enemy of Athens, founded the city of **Syracuse** on the eastern coast, which prospered amazingly. Alarmed by the growing power of the Tyrant of Syracuse, as the ruler was known, Athens dispatched an immense fleet, but it was totally defeated and some 7 000 Athenians finished up as slaves in the quarries of Syracuse.

Syracuse ruled undisputed until, unwisely allying itself with the Carthaginians against Rome during the **Second Punic War**, the city was sacked in 211 BC, inaugurating 700 years of **Roman rule**. Rome regarded the island as a convenient granary, organising the land in a series of enormous estates, the *latifundia*, which continued almost into our own time. Wealthy Romans set up 'holiday homes' on the island, thus launching the city of Taormina on its 2 000-year career as a seaside resort.

After the fall of the Roman empire in the 5C, for the next 400 years Sicily came under the control of the **Byzantine** emperors who ruled in Constantinople. Meanwhile, Arabs or Saracens from North Africa were settling on the island, first as peaceful traders and then, in the early 9C, as outright invaders. By the end of the century they were in entire control, with their capital at Palermo. As in Spain, Arab rule was beneficial, their skill in agriculture, irrigation and architecture adding to the Roman and Greek legacies.

Byzantine mosaic in La Martorana church, Palermo, depicting Christ crowning Roger II, grandson of Roger de Hauteville. Sicily enjoyed a golden period of political and cultural prosperity under his reign.

The Norman Conquest

All the previous conquerors of Sicily had at least shared a common Mediterranean background, but the Normans came like a thunderbolt from the north, led by two brothers, **Robert and Roger de Hauteville**, who had already worked their way down the length of Italy. They crossed the Strait of Messina in strength in 1061 (just five years before their fellow Normans crossed the English Channel for the conquest of England) and, after some 30 years of bitter fighting, eventually dominated all Sicily. They established a monarchy with the capital in Palermo, which endured, under five successive kings, until the last decade of the 12C.

Sicily's position, tucked away at the southern extremity of Europe, meant that it was always rather peripheral to mainstream politics. Nevertheless, over the next 700 years Germans, French and Spanish battled for possession of the island. The last Norman king, **William II**, died without an heir but his aunt had married the later Hohenstaufen emperor, Henry VII, and he established his tenuous claim with violence. His son **Frederick**, who succeeded him as emperor in 1220, is one of the great figures of European history. A multi-talented man centuries in advance of his time, running his essentially Germanic empire from this outpost in the Mediterranean, he earned for himself the sobriquet **Stupor Mundi** (The Wonder of the World). He clashed with the Pope and was excommunicated. After his death in 1250 legend told how he was seen riding at the head of a vast army into the mouth of Etna.

The Papacy interfered directly in Sicilian affairs. In 1268 a French Pope bestowed the title of King of Sicily on a Frenchman, **Charles of Anjou**. The Angevin reign was characterised by brutality towards native Sicilians, culminating in Sicily's only truly national rebellion, the **Sicilian Vespers**. A French soldier insulted a Sicilian woman and the signal for the uprising was the ringing of the bell for Vespers in Palermo, on Easter Monday 1282. The Sicilians appealed to the **King of Aragon** in Spain for aid, triggering a long-drawn-out war between Angevins and Aragonese which involved both Spain and mainland Italy.

The triskele is the ancient symbol for the 'three-cornered' island of Sicily.

Throughout the 17C and 18C Sicily declined, as sovereignty passed confusingly, and all too often bloodily, from Angevins to Aragonese, to the Habsburgs of Austria, to Bourbons ruling from Naples. **Napoleon** failed to take the island, which finally fell under British influence, the British admiral **Horatio Nelson** playing a major role. In 1860 the guerrilla leader **Giuseppe Garibaldi** defeated the Bourbon army, and in the same year an overwhelming majority voted for union with the newly-born kingdom of Italy.

Throughout all the years of oppression, it was the ordinary people, the peasantry in particular, who suffered. The dawning of the 20C showed them a means of escape: emigration. Between 1900 and 1914 a million Sicilians abandoned their homes, most making for the US.

Modern Sicily

In the 1920s and 1930s Mussolini's decree that the Mediterranean was *Mare Nostrum* (Our Sea), together with his African adventures, brought Sicily again into mainland politics. The island suffered badly in the **Second World War**, when the Allies used it as a springboard to enter Italy from Africa. The immediate post-war years were a time of confusion and feuding, with considerable violence, in which the **Mafia** played a leading role (*see* p.15). In 1946 the island was granted regional autonomy with its own president and parliament but, along with the rest of the *Mezzogiorno* (Italy south of Rome), gained relatively little from Italy's economic progress. Although Sicilians still emigrate in their thousands, land reform, the determined attack upon organised crime and a burgeoning tourist industry all give hope for the future.

PEOPLE AND CULTURE

In September 1997 the Italian government announced that a bridge was going to be built across the Strait of Messina, at last physically linking Sicily to the mainland. Even with that bridge Sicily will remain another country, with its own customs, its own art, its own cuisine and even its own language. On the mainland the people pride themselves on regionalism: Tuscans were delighted when recent DNA tests showed they were direct descendants of the ancient Etruscans. It would be impossible to gain any such result in Sicily, for it is the melting-pot of the Mediterranean, with Greeks, Phoenicians, Romans, Arabs, Normans, Germans and Spanish all contributing to the rich genetic pool. The people are Sicilians first and Italians a long way second.

Centuries of oppression by foreigners have turned Sicilians inward. They are courteous to the visitor but, unlike their mainland cousins, will not make the first move. It is unlikely that, seated in an outdoor café in Palermo or Catania, you will

Relaxing in the village of Castelmola, above Taormina.

find yourself questioned amiably by the locals as to your home, your opinion of Italy, your preference in wine, as you will in Naples or Florence or Verona.

The best description of the forces which have created modern Sicily is in the novel *Il Gattopardo* (The Leopard), by Giuseppe di Lampedusa. He spent 25 years brooding over it, then wrote it in a few months before his death in 1957. The action takes place between 1860 and 1883, the turbulent period of the revolution leading to the unification of Italy. The central character is a member of the old aristocracy, the Prince of Salina. He is treated sympathetically – the character is based on Lampedusa's own great-grandfather – but what emerges is the fantastic wealth and almost feudal power of the aristocracy compared with the grinding poverty of the peasantry. Salina has two enormous palaces in two different cities, a vast country villa and huge estate: one of the peasant families is bitterly divided over the ownership of a tiny almond grove. The story ends with an epilogue, in 1910, with the aristocratic family fading into history. Change is in the air.

The Mafia

The natural reticence of Sicilians has given this enigmatic subject an extra dimension of mystery. Significantly, the general term for it is *Cosa Nostra* (Our Thing) and it is probable that only Sicilians know the true nature of the organisation. Outside opinion ranged from the belief that there was no such thing, to a belief that it was a world-wide conspiracy against society.

The Mafia was almost certainly born of the long struggle between native Sicilians and their foreign overlords. It appears to have taken an actually criminal turn in the 19C, and in the Second World War was given a vigorous relaunch when the Allies turned to it for help in the invasion of Sicily in 1943. Links with the criminal underworld in the US were created and drug smuggling developed on an immense scale. After the murder of a number of prominent officials in 1992, the Italian government, which had been fighting the organisation since the 1920s, launched a massive campaign against leading *Mafiosis*. It has had spectacular success, but part of that success is due to the ordinary people themselves who, disgusted by the wave of violence, reacted against the Mafia.

Art and Architecture

Each of the great waves of invaders brought its own highly developed and distinctive form of art, so that Sicily's heritage is dazzlingly rich and diverse. It is also, to a remarkable degree, anonymous. Apart from the great set architectural and sculptural pieces, Sicilian art is essentially **folk art**. Highly characteristic is the vivid decoration of donkey carts with historic and mythological scenes, many of them featuring battles against the Saracens. The half-life-sized, brightly coloured **puppets** are another manifestation of this impulse, translated into drama.

The oldest surviving examples of what could be called art are the **Paleolithic drawings**, featuring both humans and animals, in the Addaura Caves on Monte Pellegrino. They have been dated to around 8 000 BC. But partly through an accident of history, partly through the nature of the

Small puppet theatres can still be found in some Sicilian cities. They usually portray Norman knights, recalling a golden age of chivalry.

medium, Sicily's prime artistic heritage is architectural.

The most spectacular **prehistoric site** is the great necropolis at Pantalica about 40km (25 miles) north-west along minor roads from Syracuse. It was in use for over 300 years, from the 13C BC to the 10C BC, and, containing over 5 000 tombs, suggests both a large and a settled population long before the arrival of the Greeks. On the Rocca behind Cefalù are the remains of an immense 6C BC cistern, which the Romans converted to their own use, and a megalithic temple.

Given the energies expended on the murderous fighting the Greeks conducted among themselves, one can only wonder at their architectural achievements which, for the most part, take the form of **theatres** and **temples**. Compared with their equivalents in Greece itself there is a subtle coarseness about them but this is compensated for by the immense strength the temples display

and the fact that they have survived in better condition. The Greeks built well. The theatre at Taormina was used by the Romans, while the temple of Athena at Syracuse was turned into a church in the 7C. The best examples of temples are at Agrigento, Segesta and Selinunte, while surviving theatres can be seen at Syracuse and Segesta.

Roman remains reflect the Romans' use of Sicily as a 'holiday resort'. In the main, they were content to adapt Greek structures, as at Taormina, but some of the most evocative **mosaics** of the Empire are to be found at Piazza Armerina.

The **Byzantine** influence was clearly great in the decoration of the churches. The great Christ Pantocrators, which dominate the apses of the cathedrals of Cefalù and Monreale, are pure Byzantine but these

Byzantine 12C mosaics in La Martorana, Palermo. The church is also known as Santa Maria dell'Ammiraglio (St Mary of the Admiral) after the Admiral of the Fleet to Roger II.

rulers left relatively little work of their own.

The next great explosion of both art and architecture occurred during the **Norman** occupation; the architectural achievements accomplished in under a century are remarkable. The dynamic behind this was a succession of ruthless but sophisticated kings who supported an extraordinary degree of eclecticism, Arab as well as Orthodox (Byzantine) elements being represented in the churches. Artistically, their prime achievements are the decorations in the Norman palace and cathedral in Palermo and the cathedral at Monreale.

Detail of some of the exquisite carvings in the cloisters of the 12C Norman cathedral at Monreale.

The **Renaissance** largely passed Sicily by. At a time when outstanding artists were almost commonplace on the mainland, Sicily could point to only one, **Antonello da Messina**, who was born in Messina in about the year 1430. He has a double claim to fame in that he was the first Italian artist to adopt the meticulous style, based on oil painting, introduced by the Flemish painters, the van Eycks. He was so successful that he worked for some time in Venice, influencing the great Bellini family with his technique. In Sicily, his best-known work is, ironically, *Portrait of an Unknown Man*, a delightful characterisation of a young man glancing sideways, half slyly, half amusedly, at the observer. It is in the Mandralisca Museum in Cefalù.

Sicilian Baroque

There is one art form which Sicily can triumphantly claim as its own and that is **Sicilian Baroque**. During the 18C, Baroque art and architecture spread throughout Europe, its flamboyant decoration symbolising the growing wealth and power of the ruling classes. In Sicily, after the immense earthquake in 1693 had devastated most of the cities in the eastern and southern parts of the island, architects, provided with a clean slate, gave full rein to their own interpretation of the new movement. Noto is an outstanding example of the new style that emerged, with every surface crammed with exuberant detail ranging from flowers and fruit to mounted horsemen and mythological creatures.

Elaborate stucco work by Serpotta, in the Oratorio di Santa Zita, Palermo.

The great Baroque sculptor **Giacomo Serpotta** (1656-1732), who was born in Palermo, specialised in elaborate façades highly ornamented with coloured marbles and stucco. His delightful plaster statues of saints and biblical stories can be found in many churches in western Sicily, especially in Palermo. His lively style was emulated by his followers, his brother Giuseppe and Giuseppe's talented son, Vincenzo Messina.

The Baroque church of San Giorgio, Módica.

MUST SEE

Deciding where to go and what to see comes down to a matter of preference in the end, but the following sights are acknowledged to be among Sicily's best, and will help the visitor to get a good feel for the island.

Cloisters at Monreale Cathedral.

Palermo Centre★★★
The heart of the island's capital city has the **Cathedral★** and **Palazzo dei Normanni★★** (Palace of the Normans) as its highlights.

Monreale Cathedral★★★
This small hill town, with wonderful views across to Palermo, is noted particularly for its cathedral's stunningly

decorated interior and 12C and 13C **mosaics**★★★.

Erice★★★
This unspoiled medieval hill-top town occupies a beautiful setting. Cobbled alleys, pretty squares and marvellous views are its main charms.

Valle dei Templi★★★
(Valley of the Temples)
Nine of the original group of ten once-magnificent temples are set on a ridge outside Agrigento. Go early to escape the crowds and to appreciate the beauty of this unique site.

Zona Archeologia, Syracuse★★★
(Archaeological Area)
These grand Greek monuments, superbly situated high above the Ionian Sea in the Neapolis (new town) area of Syracuse, were at one time part of the most important city in the Mediterranean area.

Selinus★★
Founded in the mid-7C BC, the huge, impressive remains of a Greek city, destroyed by earth-quakes, are just a stone's throw from the busy resort.

Cefalù★★
A charming seaside town, at heart a fishing port, Cefalù has a forbidding Norman **Cathedral**★★, housing some marvellous **mosaics**★★.

Taormina★★★
An up-market resort since the days of the Romans, Taormina is dramatically situated high up, overlooking the sea and facing Mount Etna. It boasts beautiful monuments, lovely gardens, and stunning views.

Mount Etna★★★
The island's highest point and one of Europe's most famous volcanoes, the still-active Etna can be ascended part-way by road and then on foot. You can see into some of the craters, where molten lava, smoking fissures and the lava landscape are an awe-inspiring reminder of the force that lies within the volcano.

Lipari Islands★★★
Otherwise known as the Aeolian Islands, this volcanic archipelago, surrounded by crystal-clear waters, is beautiful and other-worldly.

The main itinerary follows the coast clockwise from Palermo, and includes attractions and towns a few kilometres inland. Places of interest in the interior are described separately.

THE NORTH COAST

PALERMO★★★

All big cities are daunting to the newcomer
and Palermo is *big*, with a population of just
under 700 000 sprawling up the once-
beautiful valley called **Conca d'Oro** (Golden
Shell). It is not only big but rumbustious
and noisy, exhilarating but also confusing.

Happily, the ground plan is remarkably
straightforward. An immense 'high street',
several kilometres long, runs the entire
length of the city from north to south.
Beginning as the Viale della Libertà, it
narrows on entering the historic centre and
becomes the Via Maqueda. It is crossed at
right angles by another historic street, the
Corso Vittorio Emanuele, at a junction
called simply the Quattro Canti (Four

A mix of fishing boats and modern yachts jostle for space in Palermo's crowded harbour at La Cala.

Corners), also known as the Piazza Vigliena, with most of the major monuments within easy walking distance of it.

The social centre of the modern city is the immense Piazza Ruggero Settimo, dominated by the bulk of the 19C Teatro Politeama Garibaldi. Adjoining it is Piazza Castelnuovo, with the main tourist office on the west side. The office is well supplied with tourist literature: ask for the *Carta turistica* (tourist map: free) which lists bus routes, markets and monuments. Apart from its rich architecture, Palermo has some of the most important museums in Italy, which deserve more than a cursory visit.

Despite the Greek origins of its name, *Panormus* (all-harbour), referring to its splendid maritime location, Palermo enters history as a Carthaginian stronghold which was captured from the Phoenicians in the 5C BC. The Carthaginians were ousted in their turn by the Romans in 254 BC. After the fall of the Roman Empire the city passed back and forth into the hands of various invaders, until the Arabs conquered it in 831. They established their emirate there and the city became the equal in the Arab world of Cordoba in Spain and Cairo in Egypt. The Arab genius for architecture laid the foundations for the city's Golden Age, the Norman period, which began with the conquest of the city by Robert de Hauteville in 1072. During the Arab and Norman years the city was famous throughout Europe and the Mediterranean area for both its learning and its luxury, achieving its apogee under the Hohenstaufen Emperor Frederick II, Stupor Mundi, who died in 1250.

Thereafter, like the rest of Sicily, the city passed backwards and forwards between warring European dynasties, of which only the Spanish left significant traces. It came under British protection during the Napoleonic Wars and was triumphantly taken by Garibaldi and his Thousand on 27 May 1860. Palermo was heavily bombed during the Second World War but miraculously the major monuments escaped.

The itinerary that follows is oriented on the Quattro Canti.

Quattro Canti★

The name, Four Corners, exactly describes this small piazza, teeming with people and traffic. Laid out in 1608, each of its four corners has a wall fountain and a statuesque group consisting of one of the Seasons, a Spanish monarch and one of the four

One of the large 17C façades which stand at the four corners of Quattro Canti.

patron saints of the city. Nearby is **Piazza Pretoria★★** with the handsome late-15C **Palazzo Senatorio**, now the City Hall, and the fantastic **Fontana Pretoria★★**. An immense fountain with a crowd of life-size figures, it was designed in the 16C by a Florentine artist. Brides queue up to be photographed with it as a sumptuous background.

Immediately adjoining the piazza is the **Piazza Bellini★**, with one of Palermo's showpieces, the small church called **La Martorana★★**, standing on a raised platform. Also known as the 'Church of the Admiral' because it was built, in 1143, by George of Antioch, the admiral of King Roger II; it gained its present name when it was ceded to a convent founded by the Martorana family. Only the Romanesque campanile has

When the Piazza Pretoria lights up, the nymphs and monsters suddenly come to life as the water leaps and tumbles in the sparkling night of Palermo.

The 12C Norman church of San Cataldo, with its pink domes, stands beside the tall bell tower of La Martorana.

survived intact, but the treasure of the church is its lovely Byzantine **mosaics**★★ created by artists brought over from Constantinople by the admiral in 1140. In a dark corner to the right of the entrance is an almost life-size portrait of Roger II being crowned by Christ (*see* p.11). In the opposite corner is a mosaic of the admiral abasing himself before the Virgin. Sharing the platform with La Martorana is the church of **San Cataldo**★★ (late 12C), with Arabic crenellations and domes.

West of the Quattro Canti, Corso Vittorio Emanuele continues to a monumental area embracing the cathedral, the palace and a large, tree-shaded piazza. The road then continues as Corso Calatafimi to a triumphal arch, **Porta Nuova** (New Gate), which closes off the historic area. It was built in the late 16C to commemorate the triumphal entry of the Spanish Emperor, Charles V. Beyond the arch on the main road is **La Cuba**, a

The interior of San Cataldo.

The 16C triumphal arch of Porta Nuova.

country palace built for William II in 1180.

The site on which the **Cattedrale★** (Cathedral) stands has been sacred throughout Palermo's history, and Phoenicians, Romans, Byzantines and Arabs all had their places of worship on this site. On conquering the city in 1072 the Normans immediately built a church on the site of the mosque. It was completely rebuilt in 1184 and consecrated as a cathedral. The apses are still Norman although the church has Catalan-Gothic additions, including the heavy cupola. Unfortunately the Spanish gutted the interior in the 18C and refurbished it in neo-Classic style. The only important remains from the medieval period are in the first two chapels to the left of the entrance. They contain six immense porphyry **tombs** holding the mortal remains of the Sicilian royal family, including Frederick Stupor Mundi (d 1250), his mother Constance (d 1198) and grandfather Roger II (d 1154). The Roman **sarcophagus**

The original Norman Cathedral has been considerably altered over the centuries. The dome is an 18C addition.

Right: The 17C courtyard of the Palace of the Normans.

on the right contains the remains of Frederick's wife, Constance of Aragon (d 1222). Her **crown★**, found in the sarcophagus, is now displayed in the **treasury** in the south aisle.

Phoenicians, Romans and Arabs all built a fortification on the spot occupied by the **Palazzo dei Normanni★★** (Palace of the Normans), but it was the Normans who created the existing immense building, situated at the highest point of the old city. Spanish Viceroys used it for their residence, altering its appearance, and it is today the seat of the Sicilian Regional Assembly. The public entrance is at the back of the palace, facing Piazza Independenza. The **Cappella Palatina★★★** (Palatine Chapel) and the **Sala di Re Ruggero** (King Roger's Room) are highlights which should on no account be

missed for their **mosaics**, which, together
with the mosaics in the cathedrals of Cefalù
and Monreale, are the most splendid in all
Sicily, the result of a fusion of Norman,
Byzantine and Arab styles. Access to both
chambers is through a handsome 17C
courtyard and up an exterior staircase. The
Palatine Chapel is on the first floor,
overlooking the courtyard. It was begun in
1130, the year in which Roger II was
crowned as first king of Sicily, and illustrates
his religious tolerance for it draws on both
Saracen and Byzantine styles, creating a
unique combination. The wooden ceiling,
for instance, is in the form of an Islamic
mugarnas (stalactite) ceiling, common to
mosques but never before found in a
church. The mosaics created by the Saracens
also depart from tradition by including
human figures. The great Christ Pantocrator
(Ruler of All) surrounded by angels, in the

*The sumptuous
mosaics in the
Palatine Chapel of
the Palace of the
Normans are some
of the finest in
Europe.*

dome, is Byzantine. The walls are covered with mosaics of Bible stories, including the conversion of St Paul, which is best appreciated through binoculars.

King Roger's Room, on the second floor, is part of the Assembly's quarters and can be visited only in a group with a guide (free). It was originally a private chamber and has a belvedere looking out onto the Gulf of Palermo. The walls are richly covered with mosaics, but these depict hunting scenes and stylised plants that owe their origin to eastern, specifically Persian, forms.

To the south, **San Giovanni degli Eremiti★★** (Church of St John of the Hermits), founded by Roger II in 1132 on the site of a mosque, was part of an immensely wealthy abbey whose abbot was also the king's chaplain. It is now deconsecrated. On the exterior the five red cupolas are a characteristic Norman-Arab fusion. The main attraction of the church is its wonderful **garden**, a rich tapestry of citrus trees, pomegranates and brilliant flowering bushes flanked by a range of arches from the original cloisters.

The Church of St John of the Hermits is a rich mixture of Moorish and Norman styles.

North of Quattro Canti

Situated in Piazza Verdi, the **Teatro Massimo** (Greatest Theatre) is claimed to be the second largest theatre in Europe, after the Paris Opera. After being closed for many years for restoration, it was reopened in 1997.

The **Museo Regionale Archeologico★** (Regional Archaeological Museum), housed in a restored convent of the 16C and situated at the northern end of the Via Roma, is rich in finds from the Greek cities of Sicily, in particular those on the western coast. Among its treasures are the 5C and 6C **metopes★★** (sculptured panels) and an **ephebe** (youth) of the 5C from Selinunte, a bronze **ram★★** from Syracuse and **lion-head gargoyles** from Himera. There are also Roman remains: a **bronze★** of Hercules killing a deer and a priestess of Isis (2C BC) from Taormina.

Set in a rather run-down part of the city to the east of the Quattro Canti, the **Galleria Regionale della Sicilia★★★** (Regional Gallery of Sicily) is housed in the impressive **Palazzo Abatellis★**, built in 1490 in Gothic-Renaissance style. Its showpiece is the immense fresco **Trionfo della Morte★★★** (Triumph of Death), by an unknown artist of the 15C.

Despite the Arabic origin of the word *Zisa*, meaning 'magnificent' and referring to an Arabic style, the **Palazzo della Zisa★** (Zisa Palace) was built on what is now Piazza Guglielmo il Buono by the Norman king, William I, in 1160 as a pleasure palace. It houses a small museum of Islamic art.

Lying just to the south are the **Catacombe dei Cappuccini★★** (Capuchin Catacombs) with a display of some 8 000 desiccated

A close encounter with Palermitans of by-gone days...

corpses which, though impressive, is definitely not for the squeamish. The townsfolk followed the monks' custom of preserving their dead, dressed in their everyday clothes and propped up to receive pious visitors. What began as a religious custom is now a tourist 'attraction', complete with entrance fee.

AROUND PALERMO

Monte Pellegrino

At 606m high (1 993ft), the mountain towers over the city, creating a magnificent headland which the poet Goethe described as 'the finest promontory in the world'. In the **Addaura Caves★** on the northern slope are prehistoric graffiti (casts of them are displayed in the Regional Archaeological Museum). The patron saint of Palermo, Rosalia (d 1166), lived as a hermit in a mountain cave, which was turned into a

The chapel of Santa Rosalia is built into the side of the hermit Rosalia's cave.

chapel in 1625 and is known as the **Santuario di Santa Rosalia**. Festival processions make their way here in July and September.

Set in the immense **Parco della Favorita** (Park of the Favourite), on the lower slopes of Monte Pellegrino, is the **Pitrè Etnografico Museo** (Pitrè Museum of Ethnography). Founded in 1909 by Giuseppe Pitrè, the rich collection illustrates Sicilian daily life and customs. Adjoining it is the **Palazzina Cinese** (Chinese Pavilion), built in 1799 for the Bourbon King of Naples.

The Statue of Santa Rosalia, patron saint of Palermo.

Monreale★★★

Although only some 8km (5 miles) south-west of the city centre and therefore virtually a suburb of Palermo, this 'royal mount' still has the atmosphere of a small hill town. There is a charming central piazza and, just below it, a belvedere which gives a wonderful view of the Conca d'Oro, right down to the sea. The central feature is the **Duomo★★★** (Cathedral), one of the greatest works of Christian art. It was founded in 1172 by the young Norman king, William II (there is a huge statue of him, offering his cathedral to the Virgin). The entire upper half of the interior is completely covered with 12C and 13C **mosaics★★★** mostly depicting, in picture-book style, Old and New Testament stories, the story of Noah predominating. The apse is dominated by an enormous Christ Pantocrator, while the capitals of the graceful columns are carved

The intricately decorated exterior of one of the apses of Monreale Cathedral.

The interior of the Cathedral is adorned with rich mosaics illustrating scenes from the Bible.

with intricate details. The best time to see the interior is in the early evening, for although the cathedral will probably be crowded then, the westering sun lights up the mosaics beautifully. The 12C **cloisters★★★** (entrance fee), with their wonderfully carved columns, should certainly not be missed, and the terraces provide far-reaching **views★★** over the Conca d'Ora.

Mondello

This fashionable seaside town some 11km (7 miles) north of Palermo provides a much-needed green lung for the city. There are charming traces of the original fishing village, and the beach provides excellent bathing.

The popular resort of Mondello has an excellent beach, complete with an Art Nouveau pier.

Solunto★

Perched on a rocky ledge on a promontory overlooking Cape Zafferano, Solunto has a striking **setting★★**. The extensive archaeological site of **Soluntum** includes a Roman theatre and forum as well as streets, houses and a drainage system. There are extensive **views★★** across the Bay of Palermo and Monte Pellegrino.

Bagheria

Despite the sprawl of Palermo, the valley in which this small town (16km/10 miles east of Palermo) is situated has kept its citrus trees, olive groves and vineyards. During the 17C and 18C it was the summer retreat of wealthy Palermitans and some of their villas are open to the public. The most famous – or notorious – is the **Villa Palagonia★**, built in the early 18C. Its owner, the eccentric Ferdinando Gravina, commissioned some 200 grotesque **statues★** which stand in the grounds.

Statues in the gardens of Villa Palagonia, Bagheria.

CEFALÙ★★

Until the Second World War, most visitors came to this delightful little town in order to see the cathedral. Owing to the post-war development of tourism, however, it has become second only to Taormina as a popular holiday resort. Yet it has not forgotten its past as a fishing port; fishermen mend nets alongside luxury restaurants and the locals have created a touching little display of fishing techniques in the ancient **Porta Pescara** (Fish Gate).

It has a beautifully clean beach, lapped by crystal-clear water, and boasts a fine

View across the rooftops of Cefalù, with the Cathedral on the right.

setting★★. It is built on a narrow shelf between the sea and the towering bluff, **La Rocca** (The Rock), 278m (912ft) high, which gave the Greek name meaning 'head' to the town. Thanks to the demands of tourism, a splendid series of steps has been created which provide easy access to the summit of the rock. The lower part, surrounded by Byzantine walls, is shaded by pine-trees and is ideal for picnics. From it one can look straight down onto the cathedral at the foot of the rock. Dotted around are medieval, Byzantine, Roman and prehistoric remains, including a megalithic temple adapted by the Romans and dedicated to Diana, and many cisterns which keep the surface moist, even in summer. Higher up are the remains of a medieval castle which provide a panoramic viewpoint.

The town, laid out by Roger II in the early 12C, has one main street, Corso Ruggero, with narrow lanes running down to a parallel road, Via Vittorio Emanuele, which follows the coastline.

It is a puzzle as to why Roger II founded

the enormous **Duomo**★★ (Cathedral, 1131) in what would have been a tiny fishing village. It resembles a castle as much as a church, and its exterior is exactly as its Norman and Arab masons left it over 800 years ago. The only interior decoration is in the apse; the Byzantine **mosaics**★★ of Christ Pantocrator, the Virgin and angels, created in 1148, appear in dramatic contrast to the plain walls. The mosaics are the oldest in Sicily.

Piazza del Duomo, with its soaring palm trees, is the social centre of the town, with numerous cafés and restaurants. The restaurant called Domus Regia (King's House) occupies cellars contemporary with the cathedral.

Leading off the piazza is Via Mandralisca, in which is situated the important **Museo Mandralisca** (Mandralisca Museum). Founded by Baron Mandralisca in the 19C, it occupies the family home (next door are displayed the bases of oil jars of the family business). The exhibits are the pleasantly

Cefalù lit up at night, with the towers of the Cathedral and the cliffs of La Rocca dominating the town.

informal collection of a wealthy and cultured man, and include a magnificent collection of Greek vases (including the famous vase showing a fishmonger in dispute with a customer) and the fine painting **Portrait of an Unknown Man★★**, by Antonello da Messina.

On Via Vittorio Emanuele is the recently restored **Lavatoio Medievale** (medieval wash-house). Broad steps lead down to a number of shallow basins supplied with crystal-clear water from La Rocca. It may be Saracenic in origin. On the corner of Via Amendola and the Corso is the **Osterio Magno★** (Great Hostel), the remains of a medieval palace thought to have belonged to Roger II.

MILAZZO

Most tourists come to Milazzo simply to catch the ferry to the Lipari (Aeolian) Islands (*see* p.44), but there is much to be enjoyed in the town itself. It sits on a long, thin peninsula which has been continuously occupied from prehistory onwards. Greeks, Carthaginians, Romans and Spanish have all figured in the town's history. On a hill near the tip of the peninsula is the **Castello**, built by Frederick II Stupor Mundi in 1239 but considerably enlarged by the Spanish Emperor Charles V. Nearby are the remains of the 17C **Duomo Vecchio** (Old Cathedral). The **Duomo Nuovo** (New Cathedral) is in the modern part of the town and houses Renaissance paintings by Sicilian artists.

MESSINA

This great city's major claim to fame is its sheer ability to survive. Painstakingly rebuilt after the great earthquake of 1908, it was all but obliterated by cataclysmic bombing in the Second World War, when the Allied armies fought to cross the narrow Straits. It has rebuilt itself yet again and, with a population of over a quarter of a million, is Sicily's third city after Palermo and Catania. The central area is well planned with broad, tree-lined streets and attractive squares. The main feature of the city is the superb bay: a night crossing by ferry presents a spectacular view.

The **Duomo** (Cathedral), founded by Roger II in the 12C, is a miracle of reconstruction. Shattered by the earthquake in 1908 and consumed by fire in 1943, it has been restored to much of its medieval appearance, while the lower half of the façade is a survivor from the Romanesque period. The 60m (196ft)-high detached campanile (belltower) has what is thought to be the world's largest **astronomical clock★**, with moving characters.

The astronomical clock on Messina's Cathedral belltower is considered to be the largest in the world.

In the Piazza del Duomo is the beautiful **Fontana di Orione** (Fountain of Orion), an elaborate 16C Florentine work featuring Orion, the mythical founder of the city, together with various mythological figures.

Nearby, the 12C **Chiesa della SS Annunziata dei Catalani** (Catalan Church of the Virgin) is a mixture of Arab and Norman styles. It served as the chapel for Catalan (Spanish) merchants, hence its name.

The **Museo Regionale★** (Regional Museum) came into being as a repository for works of art salvaged after the 1908 earthquake, and contains work from the Byzantine period onward. It also houses a religious work by Sicily's major Renaissance artist, **Antonello da Messina**.

*Lipari (Aeolian) Islands****

These seven small islands, named after Aeolus the Greek God of the Winds, are accessible by frequent hydrofoil and ferry from Milazzo. Offering a wide range of experiences, from climbing to scuba-diving in the brilliantly clear waters of the Tyrrhenian, they are extremely popular.

The most distant island is **Stromboli*****, occupied by a still-active volcano and largely wild. The closest is **Vulcano***** with its spas and hot mud baths. Legend has it that Vulcan, the God of Fire, had his forges here. Excursions to the **Great Crater***** can be made on foot, and offer very good views (2½ to 3 hours return journey). The island's main town, Porto Levante, is just below the crater.

Lipari*, the largest island, is formed of volcanic rock and in ancient times produced obsidian, a black glazed volcanic rock. It has a completely self-contained community, centred on the small, lively town of the same name. **Lipari town*** is dominated by the old quarter,

still encircled by its 13C–14C walls. Here, the Spanish castle houses a good **museum**** where there are painted two-handled Greek vases (*kraters*) and terracotta theatrical

masks. Boat trips around the south-west coast of the island leave from Marina Corta, and the island can be toured by car. Highlights include the pumice-stone **quarries** at Canneto and Campo Bianco, and the belvedere in Quattrocchi which offers a spectacular **panorama★★★**. The island's highest point, **Monte Chirica**, is over 600m (1 974ft).

Steam and yellow sulphur on the edge of the Great Crater, Vulcano Island.

THE EAST COAST

TAORMINA★★★

The city has been a holiday resort since the days of the Greeks and Romans. Today it is probably the most popular place on the island but that need not deter you from appreciating Taormina's wonderful setting. Suspended high among the mountains, nearly 300m (986ft) above sea level, it sits in a vast amphitheatre with peaks soaring up behind it and, against all odds, has retained its medieval character. There is also an immense diversity of architecture, from the Greco-Roman theatre, with Etna as its backdrop, to the recently-built Congress Palace, with Byzantine, Saracen and Norman styles all making their contribution. It is difficult to believe that there are at least

There is a superb view across to snow-capped Mount Etna from Taormina.

Piazza 9 Aprile, with the 17C Church of San Giuseppe set among the bars and cafés.

A pleasantly shaded café in Taormina, with bouganvillea cascading down the walls.

15 large hotels tucked into the urban fabric, for they have either been converted from historic buildings (like the superb San Domenico, originally a 15C monastery) or built in one of the prevailing styles, such as the Excelsior Palace, an exuberant Gothic-Saracen pastiche dating from 1907.

Corso Umberto★ is Taormina's main street, a lively thoroughfare running right through the town from **Porta Messina** (Messina Gate) on the north side to **Porta Catania** (Catania Gate) on the south side. Attractive little lanes descend steeply from it on the east side and ascend equally steeply on the west. The Corso leads to the heart of the town, **Piazza 9 Aprile★**, which clings to the very edge of a precipice and has a stupendous **view★★**

of the sea far below. Further on is the 12C
Torre dell' Orologio (Clock Tower),
through which the Corso passes.

At the far end of Via Teatro Greco is the
magnificent **Teatro Greco★★★** (Greek
Theatre). Founded by Greeks in the 3C BC,
the theatre was almost completely rebuilt by
the Romans in the 1C AD. It provides a
splendid **view★★★** southwards towards Etna
and, from the topmost tier of seats, the
beautiful coastline with its islands and bays is
visible. It is still used for theatrical
performances. Adjoining it is the
Antiquarium, a museum containing Roman
relics.

Back in the town at the other end of Via
Teatro Greco is the **Odeon** (Roman
Theatre). The excavated section of the
theatre can be viewed from outside the
railings. More lies buried under the adjacent
Church of Santa Caterina.

*Taormina's Greek
Theatre – the
second largest in
Sicily – provides
breathtaking views
across the bay.
Plays are still
performed here in
summer.*

Almost opposite the Roman theatre is the **Palazzo Corvaja** (Corvaja Palace), a beautiful 14C palace built from black and white lava and stone. Entry is through a courtyard and up an external staircase to a large, handsome hall where the Sicilian Parliament met in 1411. It is now a tourist office and exhibition centre.

Taormina's **Duomo** (Cathedral), built in the 13C, is unusually plain and simple. In the centre of the **Piazza del Duomo** is a charming Baroque fountain (17C) decorated with mythological figures. Nearby, **Badia Vecchia** (Old Abbey), originally part of a 15C abbey, now houses the town museum.

The **Giardino Pubblico** (Public Garden), with its brilliant flowerbeds, shady trees and spectacular views out to sea, is an ideal spot to enjoy a picnic or simply while away the heat of the afternoon.

AROUND TAORMINA

Castel Mola

If you want to escape the bustle of Taormina, visit this tiny village which lies high above the town. There is a steep but pleasant winding walk up to it, or it can be reached by bus.

Mazzarò

A cable-car from Via Pirandello, just outside the town, will take you down to the beaches at Mazzarò. Although the area has been heavily developed with hotels, restaurants and tourist shops, it has been well done and there are good opportunities for swimming. A good swimmer can reach the rocky **Isola Bella**, which justifies its name, 'Beautiful Island'.

Giardini Naxos (Naxos Gardens)

The coastal road continues south to this bustling town which, today an appendix of Taormina, was in fact the first Greek colony in Sicily, founded in about 735 BC. There is an important archaeological area just west of the town, but most people come here for the excellent beaches and facilities, some of which rank as the best in Sicily.

The beaches at Isola Bella (right) and Capo Sant Andrea (left) are within easy reach of Taormina.

CATANIA★

After Palermo, this is the second city of Sicily with a population of over 400 000. First impressions are not, however, likely to be very favourable. As with so many Sicilian cities, its outskirts are a confusion, with little evidence of overall town planning. Even the historic centre is, at first sight, unattractive, for much of it is built of the black lava from Etna which virtually destroyed the city in

1669 (you can still see traces of the original lava flow just outside the city on the ring road). But Catania has a history as old and as rich as any in Sicily and there is much to be sought out.

Catania was probably founded in about 729 BC by the same Greeks who founded Naxos a few years earlier. Unlike Naxos, which is hemmed in between sea and mountain, Catania had room to develop and rapidly became one of the most important Greek towns. In the war between Athens and Syracuse it took the side of the Athenians, who used it as their maritime base, and suffered when the war was lost in 403 BC. Its citizens were sold as slaves or transported to work in the quarries of Syracuse. Catania was the first Sicilian city to fall to the Romans in 263 BC but ultimately benefited from Roman rule. It sided with Augustus Caesar in the civil war against Pompeii and was rewarded by being made a *Municipium*. In AD 253 it was the scene of the martyrdom of St Agatha, who became the patron saint of the city.

Catania's situation at the very foot of Etna means that it has suffered more than any other city from the giant volcano. The most violent recorded eruption was in 1669, when lava engulfed the city. This was followed, in 1693, by an immense earthquake. Most of the buildings post-date this period, and Catania is one of the Baroque jewels of Sicily. The city was heavily bombed in the Second World War and one of the major battles of the Italian campaign took place just outside, on the **Piana di Catania** (Plain of Catania).

The handsome boulevard of **Via Etnea★**, named after the destroyer of Catania, runs for 3km (2 miles) straight through the historic centre. Continuing as Via Caronda, it actually skirts the lowest slopes of Etna. Most of Catania's major buildings lie either along it, or a few minutes' walk away. The buildings are tall and the street relatively narrow, so it is rather difficult to appreciate the architecture; cross over and inspect a given building from the opposite side.

On the west side, standing in its own piazza, is the **University**. It was founded in 1434 by the King of Aragon and rebuilt after the 1693 earthquake. North of the university, steps lead up to the **Villa Bellini★**, which has an ornamental garden providing a much-appreciated oasis in the city centre.

The **Piazza del Duomo★** (Cathedral Place) lies at the southern extremity of the Via Etnea and is the natural heart of the city. It was designed as a unit, using dramatically contrasting black lava and white stone, by Giovanni Battista Vaccarini in the early 18C. In the centre is the **Elephant Fountain**, featuring an Egyptian obelisk placed on an ancient elephant sculpted from lava which has become the symbol of the city.

On the west side of the piazza is the handsome **Palazzo del Municipio**, the Civic Hall, also built by Vaccarini. Opposite is the **Museo Belliniano** (Bellini Museum), containing memorabilia of the musician Vincenzo Bellini, born in Catania in 1801. Almost adjoining the museum is the **Teatro Romano** (Roman Theatre), with the smaller **Odeon** beside it. They were built in the 2C and considerable remains survived both the earthquakes and subsequent building.

Founded in 1094 and rebuilt after the earthquakes of 1169 and 1693, the **Duomo★** (Cathedral) is a superb example of Baroque

The Elephant Fountain in Piazza del Duomo, Catania.

The busy fish market at Catania.

architecture. The dark pillars of the façade were taken from the Roman Theatre, while the apses were the only parts of the medieval building to survive. Among the numerous chapels inside is the **Cappella di Santa Agata** (Chapel of St Agatha), with relics of the saint which are carried on her festival day. The Cappella della Madonna houses a Roman sarcophagus which contains the ashes of members of the Aragonese royal family. The tomb of the musician Vincenzo Bellini (1801-1835) can be found against the second pier on the south side.

Just off the Via Etnea in Piazza Stesicoro, surrounded by modern buildings, is the 2C **Anfiteatro Romano** (Roman Amphitheatre). It originally held at least 16 000 spectators but it has been so ruthlessly quarried that only the bottom tiers of seats remain.

The southern end of Piazza del Duomo is closed by the **Porta Uzeda**, a handsome gateway built by Vaccarini. It leads into a

The imposing exterior of Ursino Castle which is now used as a museum.

public garden and then on to the fish market and the lively general market.

Lying just beyond Piazza Federico di Svevia is **Castello Ursino** (Ursino Castle), now used as the **Municipal Museum** and containing many archaeological finds, including good Hellenistic and Roman sculptures. This massive castle, built in the 13C for Frederick II, once commanded the coastline but the lava flow in 1669 destroyed all but the keep, cutting it off from the sea.

Piazza Dante is a pleasant little square lined with artisans' shops lying to the north-west. Its most prominent feature is the enormous **Church of San Nicolò**, claimed to be the largest in Sicily (105m/345ft long). It was rebuilt in 1735 but its façade, with gigantic columns, is unfinished. The interior is simple, almost to the point of austerity. One of the few decorative features is a meridian line on the floor of the transept, designed in 1841. Adjoining the church is a vast Benedictine monastery, with two splendid courtyards. It is reputed to be the second largest in Europe. Both church and monastery have been under restoration for some years.

MOUNT ETNA★★★

Rising to a height of approximately 3 340m
(10 984ft), the volcano is visible at a distance
of 250km (156 miles). There have been at
least 135 major eruptions of Etna recorded
in history and showers of ash are
commonplace. As recently as 1983
explosives were used to divert immense
streams of lava which were threatening
nearby villages.

*The brooding
presence of Mount
Etna dominates the
eastern end of
Sicily.*

It is possible to travel round the base of Etna on the **Ferrovia Circumetnea** (Etna Railway), which runs from Catania to Giarre. To **ascend**★★★ the volcano there are two main approaches – up the south face from Catania via Nicolosi to Rifugio Sapienza by coach or car, then on to the summit by cable-car, or up the north face via Linguaglossa from Taormina. To make the ascent on foot, it is best to go with an organised excursion or guide and to check the weather conditions on the summit beforehand, in particular the wind direction, to ascertain the direction of the permanent plume of smoke. However you go, protective clothing is advised, including strong shoes or boots, and sunglasses as the glare can be intense.

There are three main regions of the volcano itself. Its bottom third has been almost entirely covered by suburban sprawl, a process which has been slowed down substantially, if not ended, by the creation of the National Park. Above is the region of disintegrating lava, which looks like a roughly ploughed field. The crest is a wild and rather frightening area of craters and crevices, many exuding gases and a sulphurous smoke which pervades the entire area.

At the base of the volcano to the north and north-west is a beautiful area of small towns and villages set among extensive groves of orange and lemon trees.

Strange shapes, shadows and light – wading through the waters of the Alcàntara Gorges, near Taormina, is a truly fantastic journey.

SYRACUSE★★★ (SIRACUSA)

Founded by Corinthians from mainland Greece in 734 BC, Syracuse is one of the oldest, continuously-occupied major cities of the Mediterranean. It has influenced the history not only of Sicily but of Greece, Rome and North Africa. Under despotic but cultured rulers known as Tyrants, it rivalled Athens in beauty and culture and attracted some of the most brilliant minds of the Greek world, among them the dramatist Aeschylus, the poet Pindar and the philosopher Plato. Among its own illustrious citizens was Archimedes whose ingenious inventions gave much trouble to the Roman besiegers in 214 BC. Syracuse's high point came in 413 BC when it defeated a massive attack by Athenians in alliance with Catania. After an unchallenged rule of over 200 years the city finally fell to Rome in 212 BC and, though the Byzantine Emperor made the city his seat from AD 662-668, its power steadily declined.

Syracuse today falls into three main areas: the **Città Vecchia** (Old Town), on the beautiful island of **Ortigia**; the mainland; and the immense **Zona Archeologica** (Archaeological Area) on the outskirts, which contains the principal Greek remains. Despite unsightly suburban sprawl and a railway which cuts the city in two, it preserves much of its beauty, particularly along the waterfront.

Ortigia★★

The island, today connected by two bridges to the mainland, is the original settlement: a maritime people like the Greeks would naturally have been attracted to an island protected on each side by a deep-water

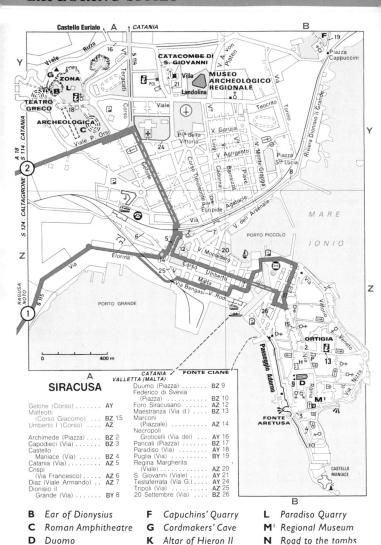

SIRACUSA

harbour. The architecture is mostly Baroque but there are considerable Greek remains. Immediately over the main bridge, for instance, in Piazza Pancali, are the massive ruins of the **Tempio di Apollo** (Temple of Apollo), probably the first Greek temple in Sicily. Today, the **Città Vecchia** (Old Town), with its wealth of Baroque and medieval buildings, is full of charming narrow streets to wander through.

The **Piazza Duomo★** (Cathedral Place) resembles a stage set designed in the shape of a boat. Around it are handsome public buildings, including the **Municipio**, or **Palazzo Senatorio**, the city hall founded on a Greek temple, and the 18C **Palazzo Benevento**. The first impression of the **Duomo★** (Cathedral) is of a purely Baroque building, for the façade was built after the earthquake of 1693. But look at it from the Via Minerva, the little street on the left, and something remarkable presents itself – the 12 massive pillars and their architraves are, in fact, part of the **Temple of Athene**. These survived the earthquake when the Norman parts of the church collapsed. Inside the cathedral on the south side are 19 more Greek pillars, their majestic mass conveying an extraordinary atmosphere of solemnity and antiquity. The temple, built in the 6C BC, was one of the richest in Sicily but was plundered by the Romans. It owed its survival to the fact that it

The Cathedral on Ortigia, apparently 18C Baroque, contains pillars from the Greek Temple of Athene.

Dream and desire, inspiration and fancy – seek and find happiness in Ortigia's ancient streets.

59

was restored in the 7C and consecrated as a church.

Not far from the cathedral, on the western side of the island, is the **Fonte Arethusa★** (Arethusa Fountain), an enchanting pool where ducks swim among papyrus. Legend has it that the nymph Arethusa was turned into a fountain to escape a pursuing god (Virgil refers to the pool in the *Aeneid*). Originally it was accessible from the sea and Nelson used it to water his fleet during the Napoleonic Wars. Leading off the square is Via Capodieci, in which is the **Galleria Regionale di Palazzo Bellomo** (Regional Museum of Medieval and Modern Art). Housed in a medieval palazzo, this is a small but important collection, concentrating on sculpture and paintings.

Castello Maniace, named after the Byzantine general who attempted to

The recently restored Baroque fountain is the centrepiece of the Piazza Archimede, at the heart of Ortigia.

reconquer Sicily in the 11C, occupies the very tip of the island and is still used for military purposes.

The Mainland

Although most of the modern development has taken place here, between Ortigia and the Archaeological Area, it includes numerous historical remains. Near the railway station are indications of the ancient **Arsenale** where warships where assembled, and in the same area are remains of the **Byzantine baths**. The park, known as the **Foro Siracusano**, is on the site of the ancient Greek *agora*, or public meeting place. Beyond the branch railway line to the west is the **Ginnasio Romano** (Roman gymnasium). Built in about the 1C, it served as a theatre.

Zona Archeologica★★★
(Archaeological Area)

Apart from the Acropolis in Athens, this group of remains to the north-west of the city is perhaps the most poignant and evocative survival from the world of ancient Greece. The setting is delightful, a mainly green area with shady trees and an attractive café – a good place to spend a hot afternoon.

The **Latomia del Paradiso★★** (Paradise Quarry) is the largest of a former group of quarries which provided the stone for the city, and where a little over 2 000 years ago 8 000 slaves were worked to death. Nothing better illustrates the fratricidal nature of ancient Greece than that these slaves were fellow-Greeks of the Syracusans, prisoners captured after the ill-fated Athenian expedition.

In the quarry, now planted as an orange

and lemon grove, is the **Orecchio di
Dionisio★★★** (Ear of Dionysius), a cave in the
shape of an earlobe. It was so named in 1608
by the painter Caravaggio because of the
legend that the cave's echo was used by the
tyrant Dionysius to overhear his prisoners'
conversations.

The **Teatro Greco★★★** (Greek Theatre),
founded in the 5C BC, was enlarged again
and again over the next two centuries, until
it became one of the largest Greek theatres
known. It was the centre of Syracusan social
life – Aeschylus performed one of his
dramas here – and the Romans later
adapted it for gladiatorial combats. The
superstructure, including the stage, was
plundered in the 16C but the immense tiers
of seats, cut into the rock of the hillside,

*The Greek Theatre
at Syracuse is one
of the largest
surviving Greek
theatres in the
world.*

survive. Just behind the theatre is **Via dei Sepolcri** (Road to the Tombs), with votive niches along the way.

On the other side of the lane is the **Ara di Ierone II** (Altar of Hieron II). This enormous altar, hewn out of the rock by the Tyrant Hieron II in the late 2C BC, was the largest in the Greek world. It was used for the public sacrifice of animals.

Next door is the **Anfiteatro Romano★** (Roman Amphitheatre). The Greek theatre proved inadequate for the Romans' taste for violent spectacles, so the Romans built this amphitheatre, the largest in Sicily, in the 1C AD.

P. Orsi Museo Archeologico Regionale★★
(Regional Archaeological Museum)

Situated just outside the Archaeological Area, in the grounds of the Villa Landolina on the corner of Via Teocrito and Via Augusto von Platen, this modern building houses the most important archaeological collections in Sicily. The exhibits come from all over the island, with emphasis on the Province of Syracuse, and present a vivid picture of the successive waves of culture. The Greek exhibits illustrate that the colonists of Syracuse maintained a deep emotional link with the mother country, for they share the same characteristics as those found in mainland Greece. The sensuous **Venus Anadiomene**, showing the goddess rising from the sea, is a Roman copy of a Greek original. The three naked *kouri* and the Hercules are pure Greek.

Near the museum are the **Catacombe di San Giovanni★★** (Catacombs of St John), among the largest today, after those in Rome.

THE SOUTH COAST

NOTO★★

Set on a gentle hillside not far from the sea, Noto is the finest pearl of the Sicilian Baroque. Unfortunately, however, it is a pearl in a considerable state of decay. Many of the buildings have been propped up with ugly scaffolding for years; care should be taken with the rest – not all the balustrades are as sturdy as they look.

When the original settlement, now called **Noto Antica**, situated about 10km (6 miles) to the north of today's town, was totally destroyed by the violent earthquake of 1693, it was decided to rebuild the town on a completely new site. Work began in 1715, and most of the principal buildings were completed by 1780. Chief of the group of architects who worked on the project was Rosario Gagliardi.

Noto is altogether one of the best examples in Europe of 18C town planning; a dramatic series of steps and terraces with spectacular views make full use of the hillside site. Its buildings are sculpted out of tufa, a delicate white stone (now mellowed to a warm honey colour) ideal for the elaborate ornamentation which characterises Sicilian Baroque. (Since 1986 the town centre has been closed to traffic, as the stone proved susceptible to the vibrations of modern vehicles.) The overall harmony of the town is impressive but the true delight here is spotting the luxuriant detail of decoration; flowers, cherubs, horses, portrait busts, masks and abstract designs proliferate.

Noto is a small town and the major buildings lie on, or just off, the main street, **Corso Vittorio Emanuele**. The Corso is

The ephemeral magic of Noto plays on the theatrical perspectives of a town reborn from its ashes – a jewel of Baroque opulence.

entered through the **Porta Reale** (Royal Gate), built in 1838 and named after the Bourbon royal house of Naples. The town rises to the right and falls away to the left, so that the impression is almost that of walking along a gallery. First, on the right, a magnificent flight of steps ascends to the rather plain **San Francesco all'Immacolata** (Church of San Francesco). Just beyond, in the Corso itself, is the more exuberant façade of **San Salvatore**, originally a convent.

The Corso leads into the great set piece of **Piazza Municipio**★. Unmistakable is the **Duomo**★★ (Cathedral), approached by a broad flight of steps. Completed in 1776, it has been closed for many years. Beside it is Palazzo Landolina, originally a private family residence. Opposite is the **Palazzo Ducezio**, now the town hall, begun in 1742, with a comparatively restrained arcaded Classical façade. Contrasting with it is the

The elegant Baroque Cathedral in Noto is fronted by an impressive flight of steps, characteristic of the town.

appropriately named **Palazzo Villadorata**
(decorated villa) in **Via Corrado Nicolaci**★, a
riot of **sculptures**★★★ supporting ornamental
balconies.

Piazza XVI Maggio has delightful gardens
shaded by monkey puzzle trees and palms.
Adjoining the gardens, behind an elaborate
fountain, is **San Domenico**★, one of
Gagliardi's churches.

The **Via Ducesi**, running parallel to the
Corso on the south, is worth exploring and
has two important churches: the Rococo
Santa Maria del Carmine in the west and
Santa Maria dell' Arco in the east. The road
terminates near pleasant public gardens.

In the upper town is another of
Gagliardi's works, the **Church of the
Crocifisso** (Crucifix), begun in 1728 but
never completed. Guarding it are two
Romanesque lions, two of the few treasures
brought from Noto Antica.

MÓDICA★

The road from Noto to Módica passes
through the region known as Ibla, a
predominantly rural landscape of
undulating open fields and drystone walls,
presided over by solid-looking stone
farmhouses.

Módica itself sits dramatically on a ridge
so steep that the town falls into two distinct
halves, **Módica Bassa** (Lower) and **Módica
Alta** (Higher), which are connected by a
tremendous flight of more than 250 steps.
Most of the places of interest are to be found
in Módica Bassa, with a number of Baroque
palaces along the Corso which traverses the
town. The oddly named **Convento dei
Mercedari** (Palace of the Rewards) houses
the **Museo Ibleo delle arti e delle tradizioni**

popolari★ (Ibla Museum of Arts and Popular Traditions), a folk museum of considerable interest illustrating the lifestyle of this distinctive region. The 15C façade of the **Chiesa del Carmine** survived the earthquake of 1693 but in the upper town, the spectacular church of **San Giorgio★★** commands an imposing position. Those who make the climb up to the church will not be disappointed, for it is one of Gagliardi's greatest works and is an outstanding example of Sicilian Baroque.

A view across Módica, with the 18C church of San Giorgio in the foreground.

RAGUSA★

There are two parts to Ragusa, the old medieval city and the new town. Spectacularly sited on a ridge with a tremendous gorge on one side, the old town was almost totally destroyed in the 1693 earthquake. Now known as Ragusa Ibla, it was rebuilt to its original plan but in Baroque style, while an entirely new city (referred to simply as Ragusa) came into being on a higher ridge to the west. It was not until 1926 that the two were united and became the provincial capital. All the modern facilities, including hotels, are in Ragusa.

Ragusa: Upper Town

Work on the **Duomo** (Cathedral) began immediately after the earthquake and was completed by 1774. The ridge slopes steeply here and the cathedral sits on a massive platform, with its richly decorated façade facing a broad terrace.

Situated by the Ponte Nuovo, the first of the three bridges over the gorge, is the **Museo Archeologico** (Archaeological Museum). Exhibits include ceramics, mosaics and a reconstructed potter's workshop, together with finds from local excavation sites, notably the Greek city of Camarina.

There is a splendid view of Ibla from the terrace of **Santa Maria delle scale** (St Mary of the Steps), at the top of the flight of steps that leads down to the old town. The church takes its name from the steps that lead up to **Santa Maria dell'Itria**, whose belltower is covered with the superb polychrome tiles of Caltagirone.

The half-deserted old town of Ragusa Ibla is based on a medieval street plan.

Ragusa Ibla★★

Today Ibla resembles a museum more than a town, for many of the buildings have been abandoned. The Mafarda area, with its deserted cottages, many half-ruinous, set against a precipice, is a ghost town and the visitor can wander at will through the narrow streets and lanes that follow the medieval configuration.

Some splendid Baroque buildings were built. Outstanding is **San Giorgio★★** in Piazza del Duomo, built in 1744 by Rosario

Gagliardi on such a scale that it is almost possible to overlook the near-life-size equestrian statue high up near the dome. **Palazzo Cosentini** has the extraordinary '**sneering masks**'★★ (*mascheroni ghignanti*) which are a recurring feature of Sicilian Baroque. Ibla has not been entirely abandoned, however. The neo-Classical **Palazzo Donnafugata**, built at the turn of the 19C, has salons decorated in the contemporary manner and houses a private art collection. Beyond San Giorgio, in Piazza Pola, is the restored **Church of San Giuseppe★**, also thought to be by Gagliardi.

The ridge and town terminate in a public garden, **Giardino Ibleo**, that is at once attractive and melancholy, for in it are three small churches, totally abandoned. Just outside the garden on the right is **San Giorgio Vecchio** (Old St George), with the remains of a 15C doorway depicting St George and the dragon.

GELA

The main reason for visiting Gela is to admire its superb **Greek remains**, as bad planning and industrialisation have spoilt much of the town. The importance of Gela in the Classical period is attested by the massive **fortifications★★** which have been uncovered under the sand dunes on Cape Soprano to the west of the city. They date from around 339 BC and some of the walls reach a height of 13m (43ft).

In the city itself is the **Museo Archeologico★** which contains the world's largest collection of the Greek painted vases for which Gela was famous. Traces of the Greek city, Acropou, have been excavated near the museum.

THE SOUTH-WEST COAST

AGRIGENTO★★★

The city was founded under the name of Akragas by colonists from nearby Gela in 581 BC, but it has escaped the same fate owing to its hill-top position and the fact that the coastline has moved outward since classical times. The lower slopes of the city are cluttered with the familiar unplanned sprawl but the medieval city on the hill escaped both the devastation of the 1693 earthquake and the attention of modern developers.

Today, Agrigento falls into two main areas: the lively city on the crest of the hill, and the wonderful Valley of the Temples about 2km (1 mile) away. Between them are modern suburbs and open country.

Medieval City

The temptation is to ignore the hill-top city and go straight to the Valley of the Temples, but there is much to enjoy here both architecturally and socially. Medieval Agrigento was built on the Greek acropolis, the citadel of Akragas which towered over the city. At its highest point is the 14C **Duomo** (Cathedral) showing a mixture of styles, including Saracen. Nearby is **Santa Maria dei Greci** (St Mary of the Greeks), built on the site of a Greek temple of 5C BC with stone taken from the temple. The narrow streets and lanes wriggle their way down to the long, elegant **Via Atenea**,

A reproduction of one of the colossal statues (telamon) from the Temple of Jupiter can be seen in the Valley of the Temples.

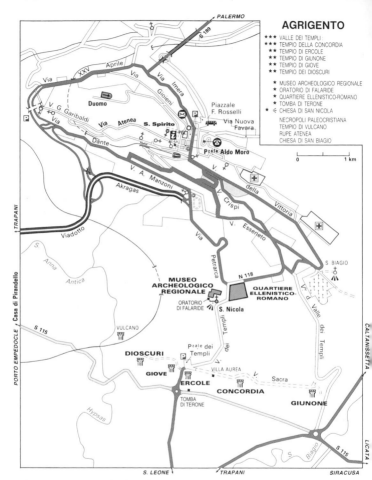

Map of Agrigento

the main street which links the medieval
with the modern town. Almost at its end,
where it enters the huge modern **Piazza
Aldo Moro**, a steep lane of steps climbs to

the 13C **Abbazia di Santo Spirito★** (Abbey Church of the Holy Spirit) where there are four delightful stucco **low-reliefs★** by Giacomo Serpotta. Beyond the piazza is the modern town.

It is possible to walk to the Valley along an attractive modern road which, descending through the suburbs, enters open country. Situated on this road is the custom-built **Museo Archeologico Regionale★** (Regional Archaeological Museum). Its artefacts, dating from prehistory onwards, are beautifully displayed. Outstanding among them are the **telamon★**, or giant, from the Temple of Olympian Zeus and the **Efebo di Agrigento★★**. Further on, on the opposite side of the road, is the excavated **Quartiere Ellenistico-Romano★** (Greco-Roman Quarter), an area of domestic buildings dating from the 4C BC.

Valle dei Templi★★★ (Valley of the Temples) This is probably the richest archaeological site in Sicily and, if possible, at least a day should be devoted to it. The setting is

The columns from the Temple of Hercules, just one of the magnificent series of temples at Argrigento.

enchanting: three unenclosed standing temples lie along a well-designed modern Strada Panoramica (Panoramic Road) among ancient olive, oleander and almond trees. Built of the same red sandstone as the ridge upon which they stand, at sunset they seem to glow, and at night are floodlit.

At the top of the Strada is the **Tempio di Giunone★★** (Temple of Juno), built in 470 BC. There is a sacrificial altar on the east side, and an ancient cistern behind it. Next comes the majestic **Tempio della Concordia★★★**

(Temple of Concord), the best-preserved temple in the Greek world, apart from the Temple of Theseus in Athens itself. The temple owes its preservation to the fact that it was transformed into a church in the early Christian era. (On the other side of the Strada is a Christian necropolis.) Finally come the columns of the remains of the **Tempio di Ercole★★** (Temple of Hercules), visible from afar and believed to be the oldest of the Agrigento temples, dating from around 520 BC.

At the bottom of the Strada is an immense area of excavation, not all of which is open to the public. The outstanding monument in the public part is the enormous **Tempio di Giove★** (Temple of Jupiter). It was intended to be the largest Doric temple of all but was left unfinished at the beginning

The sandstone of the splendidly preserved Temple of Concord takes on a warm glow in the late afternoon sunlight.

of the 5C BC. Recumbent upon it is a giant figure some 7.5m (25ft) tall, similar to the one in the Archaeological Museum and intended as a support. Further on, in the area not open to the public, four elegant columns, crowned with an architrave, break the skyline. Called the **Tempio dei Dioscuri**★★ (Temple of Castor and Pollux), the group is, in fact, a 19C reconstruction made up of various elements.

SCIACCA★

As well as being a working port, Sciacca is also a spa town whose origins go back to classical times and which contributes to its air of elegance. (In Lampedusa's novel *The Leopard*, set in the 19C, the Princess of Salina regularly visits it.)

Situated on a bluff above the sea, the upper town retains part of the enclosing walls built in the early 14C. The main entrance is through the elaborately decorated **Porta San Salvatore** (St Saviour's Gate), near which stands the Gothic **Church of the Carmine** and the 16C **Palazzo Steripinto**. Also close to the gate is the **Church of Santa Margherita** with a beautiful portal that combines Gothic and Renaissance styles.

The Corso Vittorio Emanuele, Sciacca's main street, leads to a splendid set-piece, the immense tree-shaded **Piazza Scandaliato** with wide views over the port and steps leading down to the lower town. It is the social heart of the town, where Sciacca's inhabitants come for the *passeggiata*, and has attractive cafés and restaurants. Adjoining it on one side is the Piazza M. Rossi and on the other Piazza del Duomo, all combining to make a magnificent open space. Although

founded by no less a person than the
daughter of King Roger in the 12C, the
Duomo was rebuilt entirely in the 18C.
Beyond the cathedral, approached by
narrow winding streets, are the remains of
the 14C **Castello Conti Luna**, home of one
of the powerful medieval families in Sciacca.

Situated in the lower town, in Lugomare
del Terme, the **Stabilimento Termale**
(Thermal Establishment or Spa) uses two of
the ten hot springs, one at a temperature of
32°C (90°F) the other 56°C (132°F). The
building dates from the 1920s. There is also
a natural steam cave on **Mount Kronio**,
overlooking the city to the north.

SELINUS★★ (SELINUNTE)

There could scarcely be a more dramatic
contrast between ancient and modern:
under the stimulus of tourism a small fishing
village called Marinella has expanded into a
brash modern resort, with restaurants, cafés
and hotels, but if you turn your back on the
sea and walk a few hundred metres inland
you will face the 2 500-year-old remains of
the Greek city of Selinus. Although not so
picturesque as those at Agrigento, the ruins
are on a similar scale and considerable time
should be allowed for their exploration.

Founded in about 650 BC, Selinus grew
rapidly. Its major enemy was its fellow-Greek
city of Segesta; in 410 BC Segesta allied itself
with the Carthaginians and Selinus was
destroyed, with 16 000 people killed and
5 000 taken prisoner. The survivors withdrew
to the acropolis, using the rest of the city as a
necropolis. In 241 BC they destroyed the city
themselves to prevent it falling into Roman
hands. Thereafter it was totally forgotten
until excavation began in 1823. The whole

vast area is now an archaeological park.

The main city has yet to be excavated but two areas can be visited, both approached by modern roads: the complex in the east with three temples; and the acropolis about a kilometre away, with five more temples. Rather forbiddingly, the temples are simply identified by letters – Tempio E, F, G, etc. – as it is still uncertain to which gods they were dedicated. Most are heaps of ruins but the reconstructed **Temple E** in the eastern complex stands proudly on a great platform, providing splendid views out to sea. The oldest temples lie in the acropolis complex: **Temple C**, founded in the 6C BC, is the largest and oldest of Selinus's temples and has been partially restored. The acropolis has remains of the encircling walls built by the Phoenicians, and the foundations of rows of shops. Important discoveries, including the metopes, or sculptures, which decorated the temples (the only such examples in Sicily) are now in the Regional Archaeological Museum in Palermo.

Many of the temples of Selinus have either been wrecked by earthquakes or plundered. However, Temple E has been partially rebuilt this century.

THE WEST COAST

MARSALA

This pleasant, busy town, situated on the westernmost tip of Sicily, has two modern claims to fame: on 11 May 1860 Garibaldi and his gallant Thousand landed here to begin their liberation of Italy; and in the 1770s an Englishman, John Woodhouse, realised that the sweet wine of the locality could travel well, if fortified with brandy. From then on, Marsala wine became immensely popular among the upper classes of Europe and is still the region's most important product. Some of the wine warehouses in the city welcome visitors for tastings.

One of the wine warehouse at Marsala.

The town was founded as Lilybaeum by Phoenician Carthaginians in the 4C BC, after they had been driven by the Greeks from their island settlement of Motya, further up the coast. They successfully resisted all further Greek attacks but were conquered by the Romans in 241 BC. During the Saracen period the settlement's name was changed to Marsah el Ali (harbour of Ali the prophet).

The town is built on a grid system, with its attractive main street, **Via XI Maggio**, following the original Carthaginian alignment. Leading off the street is Piazza Repubblica, with the **Palazzo Municipale** (City Hall), also known as the Loggia (begun in 1576 and completed in the early 1800s), and the **Duomo** (Cathedral). Dedicated to England's St Thomas of Canterbury, it was begun in 1628 on

Norman foundations, the façade being completed only in 1956.

Via XI Maggio terminates in the archaeologically most interesting part of the city. Known as Capo Lilibeo, or Boeo, this is Sicily's nearest point to Africa and the site of the original settlement. Excavations have disclosed Carthaginian and Roman remains. In Viale Isonzo is the **Insula Romana** (Roman Island – a block of the Roman city), with some mosaics. The **Museo Marsala** contains one of the rarest treasures of the ancient world, a Carthaginian **warship★**, probably sunk in 241 BC during one of the great sea-battles of the Punic War in which Rome broke the Carthaginian maritime dominance. Discovered off the island of Stagnone in 1969, the remains are carefully preserved. It seems to have been prefabricated and, remarkably after centuries under water, the nails are not rusty.

TRAPANI

Happily, the historic part of the town is concentrated on a long, sickle-shaped peninsula – at its narrowest point one can cross from side to side in a couple of minutes – and the extensive modern development has taken place in the hinterland.

This western coast of Sicily is the nearest to Africa, and Trapani both benefited and suffered from the fact. Founded by the Greeks who gave it the name Drepanon, from its sickle shape, it was a bone of contention between Rome and Carthage during the

The modern city stretches out behind Trapani's colourful harbour.

Punic Wars. Arabs, Normans, Angevines and Aragonese have all left their mark on the city. In the medieval period it became an important sea link between Tunis, Anjou and Aragon. Badly damaged in the Second World War, it has suffered economic decline.

The Old City★

The historic part of Trapani is easy to explore, with a pleasant public park at its eastern edge, near the 16C **Palazzo della Giudecca** (Palace of Justice), and a pedestrianised main street, Corso Vittorio Emanuele, dominated at the eastern end by the 17C **Palazzo del Municipio** (Town Hall). There is a lively fish market on the northern side.

Santa Maria del Gesù is a transitional church, built in the first half of the 16C in a mixture of Gothic and Renaissance styles and with a Catalan portal. The **Staiti Chapel** contains a glazed terracotta statue of *Madonna of the Angels* by the Florentine artist, Andrea della Robbia.

The **Duomo** (Cathedral) was built in 1635 over a church dating from the 14C. This, in its turn, had been built on a Genoese loggia, evidence of Trapani's trading importance in the 12C.

Part of Trapani's Easter mysteries procession, depicting the Crowning with Thorns.

Built in 1683 with a rich Baroque façade, the **Chiesa del Purgatorio** (Church of Purgatory) houses the famous **Misteri**, 20 groups of life-size wooden statues which are carried in one of Sicily's most important Easter processions. Representing scenes from the Passion, they were carved in the 17C and 18C by local craftsmen.

The Modern City

Originally built outside the town, the **Santuario dell'Annunziata★** (Sanctuary of the Annunciation) has been swallowed up in the modern development. The church was built between 1315 and 1332 to house a magnificent statue of the *Virgin and Child* by the great sculptor, Nino Pisano.

The **Museo Nazionale Pepoli★** (Pepoli National Museum) is housed in the convent formerly attached to the church. Founded in 1827, it contrasts with the rather run-down appearance of the town in that its exhibits are excellently displayed, using modern techniques. The archaeology section includes Phoenician, Greek and Roman remains. There are good examples of Sicilian work in the sculpture gallery, in particular *San Giacomo Maggiore* (St James the Great) by Gagini (1522).

Along the coast outside the town are the salt works that are an important part of the local economy, and the distinctive four-armed windmills typical of the region.

Two of the many windmills standing alongside saltpans to the south of Trapani.

Egadi Islands ★

Three islands make up this small archipelago which lies offshore from Trapani – **Favignana★**, the largest of the trio, **Levanzo★** and **Marettimo★**. Scuba-divers are attracted by the clear waters and numerous caves, while others come to enjoy the wild beauty of the coastlines.

The **Mantagna Grossa** range runs across the butterfly-shaped island of **Favignana★**, reaching 310m (1 017ft) at its highest. The island is noted for the traditional skills of its tunny fishermen. Between May and June a series of nets are cast out to sea and pulled in, catching the tunny which are harpooned as they reach the shore. It is a lively and fascinating spectacle to watch. The town of Favignana is

dominated by the Saracen fort of **Santa Caterina**, which was rebuilt in Norman style by Roger II. It was used as a prison in Bourbon times, and today is a high security prison. The sea has invaded the **tufa quarries** east of the town, and you will find other abandoned quarries scattered over the island. Boat trips can be taken to several of the caves aound the island, including the **Grotta Azzurra** on the west coast.

The tiny island of **Levanzo★** is usually only visited for the day as there are only track roads and no source of water. Worth a visit are the **Grotta del Genovese★**, which contain rock carvings dating from the Mesolithic period depicting dancers and wild animals. There are also cave paintings of people, animals and fish from the Neolithic period.

The greenest of the islands is **Marretimo★** and attracts those in search of tranquillity and natural beauty. The quaint little harbour has a couple of cafés (no hotel). Boat trips round the island explore the numerous limestone caves which punctuate the cliff face.

Above: Cave of Bombarda, Marretimo. Left: Levanzo.

ERICE★★★

The road from Trapani to Erice winds up the side of the only mountain on the west coast, some 750m high (over 2 460ft). From the top there is a superb view of Trapani and its bay with the Egadi Islands. The steepness of the mountain has saved Erice from the Sicilian scourge of unrestricted suburban sprawl, so that the little city (population under 1 500) is an astonishingly well-preserved medieval jewel, with a stunning **setting★★★**, where one can wander at will through cobbled streets and flower-filled gardens.

In antiquity, Erice, then known as Eryx, was famous for its shrine to Aphrodite (Venus in Latin) and acquired a particular importance to sailors, for the temple was visible from beyond the Egadi Islands.

The 12C Norman Castle at Erice provides some of the most far-reaching views on the whole island.

The campanile of Chiesa Madre, Erice, was once a medieval watchtower.

The walls encircling the triangular site are Phoenician in origin and bear inscriptions that have still not been deciphered. The usual entry is through the **Porta Trapani** (Trapani Gate), built by the Normans and leading directly into the city, but it is better to follow the Via Conte Pepoli outside the walls to the right. This route provides views of the hinterland and terminates at the 12C **Castello Normanno** (Norman Castle). It is known also as the **Castello di Venere** (Castle of Venus) for it is built on the site of the Temple of Venus, although little of that remains. Steps lead up into the remains of the castle and the gardens, beyond which it is possible to enter the town itself. The site offers far-reaching **views**★★ with, it is said, Tunisia visible in favourable weather conditions.

In the central Piazza Umberto is the
Palazzo Municipale with a museum
containing finds from the town, including a
head of Aphrodite of the 4C or 5C BC. Just
inside the Porta Trapani is a massive
watchtower of the 14C, today used as the
campanile of the adjoining Duomo or
Chiesa Madre★ (Mother Church).

CASTELLAMMARE DEL GOLFO

Most of the shoreline of the Gulf has been
taken over by holiday resorts but, although
increasingly dependent on tourism, this
principal town still has the air of a fishing
village. It stands on a bluff above the little
harbour, crowned with the remains of an
Aragonese castle. Narrow lanes run down to
the **harbour** with its fishing boats.

*The sandy beaches
and marinas of
Castellammare del
Golfo.*

PLACES TO VISIT INLAND

ENNA★

Towering up over an undulating plain in the centre of the island is an immense rock, nearly 1 000m (3 289ft) high. One would be impressed to find even a village on its summit but in fact there is a city of nearly 30 000 people. Its impressive geographical **site★★** has given it the name of the 'Umbilicus of Sicily', and Greeks, Romans, Arabs, Normans, Angevins and Aragonese have occupied it in turn.

The great **Castello di Lombardia★** (Lombardy Castle) which dominates the city was a favourite court of the Aragonese King Frederick II, where he was crowned King of Trinacria (Sicily) in 1314. His queen,

Enna occupies a lofty site overlooking the centre of the island.

There are spectacular views over the island from the towers of Castello di Lombardia, Enna, where Frederick II was crowned in 1314.

Eleonora, founded the **Duomo** (Cathedral) in 1307. Damaged by fire in the 15C, the castle was largely rebuilt in the 17C and the **interior★** is a riot of Baroque style. There is much outstanding woodwork, including the walnut ceiling carved in 1573 and the splendid *casciarizzo* (cupboard) in the vestry, carved with scenes from the life of Christ. From the top of the tallest of the six remaining towers (there were originally 20) the **views★★★** are exceptional.

To the south-west, situated in a public garden, is the isolated **Torre di Federico II★** (Frederick's Tower), probably part of the defences built at Enna by Frederick II. The tower is said to be in the centre of the island.

PIAZZA ARMERINA

This pleasant little hillside town lying directly south of Enna is worth a visit in its own right. The **Duomo** (Cathedral) at the highest point of the city is 17C Baroque, although the campanile is a survivor from the original 15C Catalan building. The

Church of Sant'Andrea, some way out of the town centre, is early-12C Norman.

The main reason for coming here, however, is to see the sumptuous mosaics of the **Villa Romana del Casale★★★** (Roman Villa of Casale) in the small hamlet of Casale. Set in a green valley about 6km (4 miles) south-west of Piazza Armerina, the villa was built in the 3C-4C BC, and was evidently the home of a wealthy and powerful family for it continued to be occupied until at least the late 5C. Subsequently, it was completely forgotten until the 18C and organised excavations (still in progress) did not begin until the 1930s.

The villa consists of a number of rooms and complexes, including a bathhouse and basilica, arranged around a great central peristyle resembling a cloister. Set in a well-tended garden, the villa is extremely well laid out. A transparent roof covers most of

One of the mosaics showing the Great Hunt, in the Villa Romana del Casale.

the remains and an intricate series of walkways takes the visitor actually over the mosaics, which are of African-Roman style, like those in Tunisia. Their quality and number are quite astonishing and adequate time should be allowed for the visit. A particular favourite is the mosaics of girls performing gymnastic exercises while wearing engagingly modern 'bikinis' in the **Sala delle Dieci Ragazze** (Room of the Ten Girls; *see* p.121).

The mosaics of the Great Hunt show a tremendous series of hunting activities on the floor of a long central corridor. The action is presumably taking place in Africa, for the game includes ostriches, elephants and tigers. By contrast there are the charming mosaics of the Little Circus, depicting children playing with dolphins and winged cupids fishing.

CALTAGIRONE★

Situated at a crossroads on the main road running across the island from Catania to Gela, the town has always been of strategic importance and was settled well before the Greeks arrived. However, as a victim of the 1693 earthquake, its buildings and monuments are predominantly Baroque. Caltagirone is visible from afar, for it is built on three hills, its buildings sweeping down into the plain, like the skirt of a robe.

On ascending to the upper town the visitor is immediately reminded of Caltagirone's chief industry – ceramics – by the richly decorated balustrades of the bridge carrying the main road between two crests of the hills. Even more dramatic, however, is the tremendous flight of steps – **La Scala★** – which rises from the Municipio

Caltagirone, viewed from one of the three hills on which the town is built.

to the **Church of Santa Maria del Monte**. Begun in 1606, the steps took 10 years to complete. Each riser features a different design in ceramics which gleam in the sun; they are lit with some 4 000 coloured lamps to celebrate the 25 July festa of San Giacomo.

All around La Scala are small shops where you can see every stage in the manufacture of ceramics. The **Museo della Ceramica** (Ceramics Museum) is set in a pleasant **garden★** decorated with ceramic tiles and objects. Most of the other interesting buildings are in the upper town, including the Baroque **Duomo** (Cathedral), rebuilt in the 19C, and the **Corte Capitaniale** (Captain's Court), elaborately decorated by the Sicilian sculptors, the Gagini brothers.

PALAZZOLO ACREIDE

Situated due south of Etna and more or less level with Syracuse, the modern town was largely destroyed in the 1693 earthquake and as a result the major buildings are mostly Baroque, except for the Municipio of the 19C. In 1971 a dedicated scholar, Antonino Uccello, founded a folk museum in the **Casa Museo** which, after a difficult start (it was closed for many years), has developed into an important collection. The eclectic collection includes puppets, olive-presses, household items, ceramics, and much more.

The other major interest of the town lies in the **archaeological zone★** on the ridge a short distance to the south-west. Here the ruins are the remains of the Greek city of Akrai, the first colony founded by the Siracusans in 664 BC, and include a theatre of the 3C BC, the senate house and a temple of Aphrodite of the 6C BC. Particularly interesting are the rock reliefs carved in the quarry which provided stone for the city. They are related to the fertility goddess, Cybele.

The Greek Theatre at Segesta is built into the hillside. The Gulf of Castellammare can be seen in the distance.

SEGESTA★★★

High up in the hills in the north-west corner of the island, far from any modern development, with the sound only of the wind and the cicadas, the great Greek **Tempio★★★** (Temple) and its accompanying **Teatro★** (Theatre) is one of the most poignant sights in the Mediterranean. The temple was begun in the austere Doric style in the late 5C BC. The theatre of the 4C BC lies further up the hill, built into the crest and so providing superb **views** for miles around. The two buildings are all that is left of the city of Segesta which, as an ally of the Carthaginians, was endlessly at war with Selinunte on the coast to the south. Eventually it fell to the Romans and was abandoned shortly afterwards.

The impressive Greek temple at Segesta is one of the finest in the Mediterranean.

93

WEATHER

Until the 1950s Sicily was essentially a winter resort. Traditionally, holidaymakers from northern Europe would come down around November and leave in April or May, before the blast of summer. Mass tourism has meant that visitors are catered for throughout the year but, if you can possibly do so, avoid July or August when temperatures often reach 30°C (87°F). Sicily, after all, is barely 144km (90 miles) from Africa and in the high summer the heat can be intolerable: the

In spring the countryside is full of colour before the heat of high summer sets in. This is a view of Caltabellotta, near Agrigento.

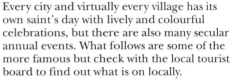

land is burnt brown and everyone goes to earth between noon and 3pm. The end of September and October can bring torrential rains, although these spells are short-lived. Undoubtedly the best time to visit Sicily is in spring, when orange and lemon trees are laden with fruit and large stretches of the country are veiled in almond blossom. The temperature is a pleasant 21°C (70°F), rising to 24°C (76°F) in May, and the flowers and countryside are at their best.

CALENDAR OF EVENTS

Every city and virtually every village has its own saint's day with lively and colourful celebrations, but there are also many secular annual events. What follows are some of the more famous but check with the local tourist board to find out what is on locally.

January
All over Sicily (6 January): Epiphany festivals.
Piana degli Albanesi: Epiphany celebrated according to the Orthodox rite.

February
Agrigento (1st week): Festival of the Almond Trees in Blossom, held in the Valley of Temples.
Catania (1-5 Feb): St Agatha's Day, with procession of decorated floats and giant candles.
Carnival (week before Lent): Some of the best are in Acireale, Sciacca, Taormina, Trapani, Giardini-Naxos and Paterno.

April
Holy Week: Celebrations are held in towns and villages all over the island. Of special note are those in Enna, Messina, Ragusa, Agrigento, Prizzi, Piana degli Albanesi and

Trapani. They include colourful processions of floats carried by costumed participants, dancing, and performances of the Passion Play and the Mysteries.

May
Ragusa: St George's Martyrdom.
Taormina (end May): Local folklore display, with painted carts, puppets and costumes.

June
Palermo (June-September): Music festival at Villa Castelnuova.
Messina (3 June): Festival of Madonna della Lettera.

July
Palermo (10-15 July): Celebrations in honour of St Rosalia.
Caltagirone (24-25 July): *La Luminara* – illumination of Santa Maria del Monte stairway.
Trapani (all month): Outdoor opera at Villa Margherita.

Nearly every town or village has its own festival, complete with colourful processions such as this at Giarre, near Taormina.

August

Piazza Armerina (13-14 August): Norman Conquest celebrations, with jousting.

Syracuse (1st Sunday): A historical boat race around Ortigia.

Messina (14 August): Parade of the Giants, the mythical founders of the city.

September

Calascibetta (6-7 Sept): *Sagra di Buon Ripaso* – food and folk festival, with horse racing, sausage feasting and livestock fair.

Caltanissetta (29 Sept): Feast of St Michael the Archangel.

October

Zafferana Etnea (all month): Feasting on local produce – grapes, mushrooms, honey, wine and chestnuts.

November

Palermo (1 Nov): Celebration of the Dead (or All Saints), with toy fair.

December

Syracuse (13 Dec): Festival of St Lucia.

ACCOMMODATION

For information before you go on all aspects of staying in the region, refer to the *Michelin Red Guide Italia*. The guide, which is updated every year, offers a selection of hotels, from the simplest to the most luxurious, classified by district and according to comfort.

The Italian government classifies hotels from one to five stars. Prices vary with the supply and demand in a particular area. Outside the main resort areas the standard of accommodation is usually lower than equivalent hotels elsewhere in Europe. Some hotels are open only during the high season. In rural areas, places to stay can be few and far between, so it is advisable to book ahead.

Average prices per double room, with bath
5 star: over L500 000
4 star: L300-500 000
3 star: L200-300 000
2 star: L100-200 000
1 star: under L100 000

A popular alternative to hotels in Italy is *Agriturismo*, self-catering (usually) accommodation on a working farm. This is officially illegal in Sicily as yet but is accepted in practice. Home-grown produce is often available and prices are reasonable. For further information contact the head office at Corso V Emanuele 101, 00186 Rome, ☎ **(06) 651 2342**, or the Associazione Regionale Agriturist, Via A D Giovanni, 14, Palermo ☎ **(091) 296 666** (*see also* **Tourist Information Offices**, p124).

There are six youth hostels, *ostelli della gioventù*, in Sicily. For details of hostels and how to book, apply to the Italian Youth Hostel Association (AIG) at Via Cavour 44, 00184 Rome ☎ **(06) 4871 152**.

Recommendations

Over 400 000
Taormina
San Domenico Palace (Piazza San Domenico 5 ☎ **(0942) 237 01** Fax 62 55 06) This convent dating from the 15C has been converted into a luxurious hotel (102 rooms) renowned for its spectacular views of the coast and Etna. Heated pool and garden.
San Giovanni La Punta
Villa Paradiso dell'Etna (Via per Viagrande 37 ☎ **(095) 751 24 09**) Fax 741 38 61) Very comfortable hotel (35 rooms) with heated pool in the garden.

210 000–400 000

Agrigento

Colleverde Park Hotel (Via dei Templi
☎ **(0922) 295 55** Fax 290 12) Nice,
comfortable hotel (48 rooms) with views of
the Valley of the Temples.

Baglio della Luna (Contrada Maddalusa
☎ **(0922) 511 061** Fax 598 802) This
charming hotel, installed in a renovated
watchtower, is noteworthy for its superb
views of Agrigento's famous Greek temples.

Panarea (Aeolian Islands)

Cincotta (98050 Isola Panarea
☎ **(090) 98 30 14** Fax 98 32 11) Small and
quiet hotel (31 rooms) with swimming pool
and views of the nearby islands.

Syracuse

Grand Hotel (Viale Mazzini 12, in the Città
Vecchia ☎ **(0931) 46 46 00** Fax 46 46 11)
Comfortable hotel (39 rooms). Meals served
on the panoramic terrace.

190 000–250 000

Catania

Garden (95030 Trappeto ☎ **(095) 717 77 67**
Fax 717 79 91) This comfortable and large
hotel (approximately 100 rooms), with
garden and swimming pool, is situated
4km/2.5 miles north of Catania (Etna-San
Gregoria exit from the Catania Nord
motorway).

130 000–200 000

Castel di Tusa

Grand Hotel Atelier sul Mare (Via Cesare
Battisti 4 ☎ **(0921) 33 42 95** Fax 33 42 83)
Nice hotel with rooms decorated by
contemporary artists. Meals available for
guests only.

Giardini-Naxos

Arathena Rocks (Via Calcide Eubea 55 ☎ **(0942) 51 349** Fax 516 90) Very comfortable hotel (49 rooms) offering numerous amenities (swimming pool, garden, tranquil setting, pleasant views). Half board only.

Nicolosi

Corsaro (Piazza Cantoniera Etna Sud ☎ **(095) 91 41 22**) Quiet and secluded situation.

Palermo

Villa Igea Grand Hotel (Salita Belmonte 43 ☎ **(091) 54 37 44**) Villa built at the beginning of the century; meals served in the garden.

Ragusa

Eremo della Giubiliana (Contrada Giubiliana ☎ **(0932) 66 91 19**) Nice hotel in a pleasant and calm setting; meals served in the garden.

Syracuse

Domus Mariae (Via Vittorio Veneto 76 ☎ **(0931) 248 54** Fax 248 58) Small hotel (12 rooms) conveniently located in the Città Vecchia.

Carlentini

Casa dello Scirocco (Contrada Piscitello ☎ **(095) 783 44 85**) Rural accommodation (Agriturismo).

FOOD AND DRINK

Sicilian food reflects its diverse ethnic origins and has a long history of excellence. Given a head start with plentiful local natural ingredients such as fresh fruit and vegetables, groves of almonds and olives, and abundant seafood including tuna, mullet, swordfish and sardines, the ancient

Greeks became known for their creative dishes, and down through the Middle Ages the island remained synonymous with fine cuisine.

The Arabs brought with them their own distinctive style, and many of today's common ingredients – aubergines, rice, citrus fruits, capers – were introduced by them. They also brought the rich sweets and desserts to be found all over the island.

Some Specialities

Zuppa di verdura (vegetable soup) comes in an almost solid form and the rice-based dishes (*risotto*) and most **pastas** are sufficient for a main course. Perhaps the most

Pavement cafe, Taormina.

ubiquitous pasta dish is *spaghetti alle vongole* (with baby clams), though you will find pasta with other seafood such as lobster, crayfish and sardines (*pasta con le sarde*). *Pasta alla Norma* is a delicious blend of aubergines, tomato sauce, basil and ricotta cheese, and *pasta ca'anciova e muddica* combines anchovies with tomato paste. The Arab influence is particularly noticeable in the north and west where *couscous* will invariably appear on the menu.

Fish and seafood play a prominent role all round the island. *Zuppe di Cozze* (mussel soup) is not really a soup at all but steamed mussels in a sauce. *Spada* (swordfish) is usually grilled with lemon, olive oil and oregano, or cooked with a sauce (*salmorigano*), or rolled with a filling of breadcrumbs, onions and spices (*involtini*). Squid (*seppia*) is also a Sicilian speciality.

Meat dishes are often based on veal, and sausages made from veal or pork come in various forms and sizes. Vegetables usually form an important part of any meal and often feature as hors d'oeuvres (*antipasti*). Aubergines, tomatoes, peppers and courgettes are particularly good.

Desserts are usually sweet and are often made with the almonds which grow so prolifically on the island. Fruit, honey and ricotta cheese are also widely used in sweets, cakes and pastries, most of which are not for those watching their waistlines! *Cassata*, a cake made from ice cream or ricotta cheese, almonds and candied fruit, is an extremely rich Arab-influenced speciality. Or try the famous *cannoli* – brandy biscuits filled with fresh ricotta, chocolate chips and candied fruit. Of course, the home-made Sicilian ice creams (*il gelato*) should not be missed.

A savoury bottargua of tuna eggs served with fresh pasta, the speciality of Favignana, the tuna fishermen's island – a simple but unforgettable meal.

Mealtimes

A *trattoria* is a smaller, simpler establishment than a *ristorante*, though the food and service are often just as good.

Breakfast (*prima colazione*) tends to be a sketchy affair: ask for *caffè con latte* (coffee with milk) if you want a good cup of coffee; otherwise you finish up with a small, sweetish drink called *cappuccino*.

The **midday meal** (*pranzo*) is the main meal of the day and traditionally has five parts: *antipasti*, a mixture of starters; *il primo*, the first course consisting of pastas and soups; *il secondo*, the second or main course, consisting of fish or meat; *contorno*, vegetables; and finally, *dolci*, dessert. Sicilians normally eat at least three courses, but you are perfectly at liberty to chose only one course – for example to have a starter as main course, though you will be charged more for it.

The **evening meal** (*cena*) follows the same pattern as *pranzo*.

Snacks

There is a wide range of fast food and snacks available in Sicily, and you will find bars, *rosticceria*, *gastronomia* and *tavole calde* serving hot or cold snacks that will satisfy healthy appetites. *Pizzerie* serve a range of excellent pizzas, cooked in hot ovens at the back (they often only serve during the evenings as it is too hot during the day).

Bars and cafés range from the unpretentious, dark room off a side street, where the locals meet for a chat, to the luxurious street cafés aimed at the tourist trade. All serve coffee (*espresso*, *cappuccino* or *caffè con latte*), and many offer croissants (*cornetti*) or other pastries for breakfast.

After a long morning sightseeing, stop off for a refreshing *granita* (flavoured ices), *caffè freddo* (iced coffee), *thè freddo* (iced tea), cold drinks or ice cream.

Drinks

Local **wine** (*vino locale* or *vino da tavola*), often served in jugs straight from the barrel, is cheap and excellent, light and dry to the taste. Bottled wine is more expensive, although still good value; prices in Taormina are likely to the highest you'll find. More discerning drinkers will want to try some of the local wines, a number of which have attained the DOC accreditation (*Denominazione di Origine Controllata*): *Corvo* (dry, fruity white or a strong red) from the north coast; *Etna* (dry whites, lusty reds and rosé), grown on the slopes around Mount Etna; and *Cervasuolo di Vittorio* (red or white) from Ragusa province.

Locally produced liqueurs and marmalades.

Dessert wines are good in Sicily. The most famous, of course, is **Marsala**, which is made by fortifying a base wine with grape brandy, and then ageing the wine. There is a wide range of Marsalas, from the very sweet to quite dry, and from aged to young wines. Though mainly produced on the west of the island, look out for variations around the mainland and on the smaller islands.

Internationally branded **spirits and liqueurs** are readily available, although the Italian versions (*nazionale*) are cheaper.

Recommendations

The following are restaurants which the author has particularly enjoyed:

Acireale
La Bettola dei Marinai (Via Canale Torto 34 ☎ (095) 876 352)

Agrigento
Leon d'Oro (☎ (0922) 41 44 00) Nice restaurant located 7km/4 miles from Agrigento in the town of San Leone; closed Mondays and from 20 October to 15 November.

Augusta
Donna Ina (☎ (0931) 98 34 22) This restaurant, specialising in seafood dishes, is located in the village of Faro Santa Croce, 6.5km/4 miles from Augusta; closed Mondays.

Caltagirone
La Scala (Scala Maria SS. del Monte 8 ☎ (0933) 577 81) Simple restaurant offering menu for less than 30 000L.

Casale
There is only one restaurant in this tiny hamlet, but happily it is a good one.

Catania
La Siciliana (Viale Marco Polo 52/a ☎ (095) 37 64 00) Located along the busy Viale Marco Polo to the north of Catania's historic centre, this restaurant offers summer dining in a pleasant garden; closed Sunday evenings, Mondays and from 12-18 August.

Cefalù
Here one is spoilt for choice, with a number of good alternatives. Two good options are **La Giara** in Via Vetinari, which has a roof terrace with spectacular views over the city, and **Lo Scoglio Ubriaco** on Via Carlo

Ortolani, which also has a delightful terrace, this time overlooking the sea.

Lipari (Aeolian) Islands
E Pulera (Via Diana ☎ (090) 981 11 58) Pleasant restaurant serving local island cuisine under a refreshing flower-bedecked pergola. Advance reservation is recommended.

Letojanni
Da Nino (Via Luigi Rizzo 29 ☎ (0942) 65 10 60) Restaurant (also with rooms); seafood a speciality.

Milazzo
Al Castello (Via Federico di Svevia 20 ☎ (090) 928 21 75)

Noto
Trattoria del Carmine (Via Ducezio 1/a)

Palermo
Trattoria Biondo (Via Carducci 15 ☎ (091) 58 36 62) Closed on Wednesdays and from 15 July to 15 September.

Il Vespro (Via B D'Acquisto 9 ☎ (091) 58 99 32) Restaurant and pizzeria; closed Mondays and August.

U'Saracinu (Via del Convento 9 ☎ (0932) 24 69 76) Restaurant offering good value; closed Wednesdays.

Pizzeria Bellini (Piazza Bellini, by La Martorana Church) One of the few outdoor restaurants in Palermo; in bad weather there is a pleasant room upstairs (they also do take-aways).

Il Grande Albergo Sole (almost on the corner of Quattro Canti) Despite its name, this restaurant serves modestly priced meals.

Just beyond Arca Nuova, in Piazza Independenza, a small open-air buffet serves a wide range of individually-cooked quick food.

Syracuse
Jonico-a Rutta e Ciauli (Riviera Dionisio il
Grande 194 ☎ **(0931) 655 40**) Enjoy typical
Sicilian dishes from a terrace affording views
of the sea and the rocky coastline; closed
Tuesdays.

Taormina
San Domenico Palace (Piazza San Domenico 5
☎ **(0942) 237 01**) If you find yourself here at
the end of the holiday with lire to spare,
then splash out at this superb restaurant, in
a luxury hotel (*see* p.98).

Trapani
Taverna Paradiso (Lungomare Dante
Alighieri 22 ☎ **(0923) 223 03**)

Trecastagni
Villa Taverna (Corso Colombo 42
☎ **(095) 780 64 58**) Nice little restaurant,
typical atmosphere.

SHOPPING

Like mainland Italy, Sicily
maintains the tradition of the
small artisan making and
selling his own wares. Even the
ubiquitous **puppets** are
handmade. In his tiny *bottega*
(shop) at 445 Via Vittorio
Emanuele in Palermo, Vicenzo
Argento creates his *marionette*
from wood to a spectacular
finish.

   Ceramics are to be found
everywhere, the widest range
and best selection being in
Caltagirone, where again you
can watch the process from
start to finish.

   Mosaics are not quite so

*Sicilian ceramics
are usually of good
quality and
reasonably priced.*

common but, in a workshop almost adjoining the cathedral at Monreale, a *mosaicista* and his assistant are carrying on the centuries-old tradition of creating designs from minute pieces of stone. Taormina has on display articles made from Etna's **lava**, some items of quite remarkable vulgarity, others of considerable beauty.

Coral and gold **jewellery** is made on the island, with the top-quality pieces being sold in Palermo, Catania and Taormina, although cheaper items can be found in most resorts.

Palermo's **markets** are famous for their size and variety. Just south of San Domenico, on the Via Roma, is a warren of narrow streets totally taken up with stalls. Here you will find an amazing range of Italian pickled, spiced and dried foods, with olives in bewildering variety and red chillies hanging like ornaments.

Pasticcerrie (pastry shops) offer an equally bewildering variety of *dolce*, cakes and tarts which are almost a work of art in themselves. Sicily has one great speciality bequeathed to it by the Arabs: elaborately sculpted and coloured fruit made from almond paste and known as *Martorana*. These sweets also come in the shape of fish – rather disconcerting, for the taste is uniformly sweet.

ENTERTAINMENT AND NIGHTLIFE

In addition to the **religious festivals** with their processions, music and fairs, there is a wide range of sophisticated entertainment on the island, including **opera**, **symphony concerts** and **ballet**. It is worthwhile visiting the local tourist offices to find out details of performances.

A concert in the church of Santa Maria dello Spasimo, in Palermo – the music swells to reach the starry dome above.

Preparing for a concert in the splendid Baroque surroundings of San Bartolomeo Cathedral, Lipari.

The Teatro Massimo in Palermo, after being closed for many years, again offers an impressive summer programme of **music**. The various **Greek theatres**, including those at Tindari, Syracuse, Segesta and Taormina, put on **classical and modern drama** in quite magical settings. Taormina's International Art Festival, running from July to September, is the most comprehensive in Sicily, embracing cinema, drama, dance and music. Catania also has a summer music festival. There are **cinemas** in the major cities.

The entertainment unique to Sicily, however, and which should not be missed, if at all possible, is the **puppet theatres**. They have been popular with Sicilians since at least the 14C and their stories follow a strictly traditional form, mostly based on the legends of Charlemagne and his supposed battles with the Saracens. Don't worry if the dialect is impenetrable, for the action is easy to follow, usually ending up with a gory fight in which heads are realistically lopped off. The beautifully designed puppets, although only knee-high, present the remarkable illusion of being life-size. Two of the best

The clear waters around the coast of Sicily attract scuba divers from all over Europe. This is Preveto, off Favignana, one of the Egadi Islands.

theatres are the Teatro Don Bosco, in Viale Mario Rapisardo in Catania, founded in 1921, and the Teatro de Pupi in Cortile Manin, in Monreale, where such delights as 'The destruction of Troy', the 'Destruction of Agrigento' and 'Orlando Furioso' are offered on Sundays.

SPORTS

Owing to its numerous lakes and rivers and lovely varied coastline, **swimming** is one of the obvious activities to enjoy on Sicily. Pollution can be a problem on the mainland, however, especially around the Gela Riviera, Augusta and Termini Imerese. The islands offer some of the cleanest beaches. Other watersports include **windsurfing** (best on the south coast), **diving** (favourite areas being the Egadi Islands and Taormina) and **sailing** (particularly around Palermo).

A less obvious choice of sport in summer is **skiing**; Mount Etna is often snow-capped and the main resorts are at Linguaglossa on the northern side and Nicolosi on the southern side. The main ski season runs from December to April. Joining a **hiking** trip is another way of seeing Mount Etna at close quarters but always go with a guide: details from the tourist offices. Less strenuous walks can be enjoyed around the coasts of the Aeolian Islands or in the nature reserve of Lo Zingaro on Capo San Vito, Palermo Province.

A relatively new addition to the Sicilian sporting scene is **horse-riding** and there are now a number of stables dotted around the island; details can be obtained from tourist offices.

THE BASICS

Before You Go

Visitors entering Italy should have a full passport valid to cover the period in which they will be travelling. No visa is required for members of EU countries. Citizens of Republic of Ireland, the US, Canada, Australia and New Zealand can stay in Italy for up to three months without a visa. No vaccinations are necessary.

Getting There

By Air: Sicily has two main international airports, at Catania in the east (Fontanarossa) and Palermo in the west (Falcone e Borsellino). There are several direct charter flights to Sicily from the UK. There are daily direct scheduled flights from Gatwick to Palermo, with a stopover in Florence, operated by Meridian ☎ **(020) 7839 2222**. Other flights go via Rome and are operated by Alitalia, ☎ **(020) 7602 711** and British Airways, ☎ **0345 222111**. There are direct flights from New York in the US to Palermo, and to Milan and Rome with connections to Sicily.

By Car: To take a car into Italy, a vehicle registration document, a full driving licence and insurance papers are required. Travelling from the UK is expensive (London to Palermo is about 2 700km/ 1 687 miles and will take several days). Motorway tolls and the ferry across to Sicily must be added to the cost of petrol and overnight hotels. Fly-drive options are also possible. *See also* **Driving** and **Car Hire**

By Coach: Eurolines runs regular bus services to Rome and other Italian cities from the UK and other European countries. From there you will have to proceed by another coach or train. Information and bookings in the UK from 52 Grosvenor Gardens, London SW1W OAU ☎ **(020) 7730 8235**.

By Ferry: Ferry services operate from Genoa, Livorno and Naples to Palermo. This cuts out the long drive through Italy if you are taking your car. Bookings can be made at the Italian Tourist Office.

By Train: Travelling by train from Britain is a long haul (40-odd hours, sometimes more) and is certainly no cheaper than flying but it is possible and the line passes through some beautiful countryside. Overnight services with sleeping compartments are available. A number of routes can be taken, which will affect the price, and various discounts are available for those aged under 26.

For further information contact Rail Europe enquiries, Victoria Station, London SW1 ☎ **(020) 7834 2345**; or the CIT office which acts as an agent for Italian State Railways and can be contacted at:
UK Marco Polo House, 3-5 Lansdowne Road, Croydon, Surrey ☎ **(020) 8686 0677**.
US 342 Madison Avenue, Suite 207, New York, NY 10173 ☎ **(212) 697 2497**.

Arriving

Within three days of arriving in Italy, all foreign nationals must register with the police. If you are staying in a hotel, the management will normally attend to this formality but strictly speaking the visitor is responsible for checking that it has been carried out.

From Palermo airport there is a regular bus service run by a private company to and from Palermo's main station; the journey takes about 45 minutes. Timetables, which vary according to the season, are displayed at the airport and the station.

From Catania airport, buses (no 24) run regularly to and from the main station, but generally operate between 5/6am and 10/11pm.

Taxis levy an additional charge for airport trips but are readily available.

Panarea, the smallest of the Lipari Islands, has a relaxed atmosphere.

A-Z

Accidents and Breakdowns

In the case of a breakdown, dial ☎ **116** from the nearest phone box and the operator will send an ACI (Italian Automobile Club) service vehicle. A red warning triangle should be placed 50m (165ft) behind the vehicle and hazard warning lights switched on. In the event of an accident, exchange names, addresses and insurance details. To contact the police or ambulance, dial ☎ **113**. There are emergency telephones at 1km (0.6 mile) intervals along the motorways (*autostrade*).

When travelling in a hire car, contact the rental firm in the event of an accident or breakdown.

Should you need them, spare parts and service facilities for Italian makes of cars are simple to find but all major towns have agencies for most other makes. *See also* **Driving**

Accommodation see p. 97

Airports see Arriving p.113

Banks

Banks are open 8.30am–1.30pm, Monday to Friday, and sometimes for one hour in the afternoon, usually 3–4pm. They are closed at weekends and on national holidays. A passport or identification is required if you are changing money, and note that you should allow plenty of time to make a transaction.

Tourists can change money at main railway stations and airports; travellers' cheques and cheques can be changed at most hotels, although the exchange rate may not be very favourable.

Bicycles

Cycle-hire shops are not widespread in Sicily and in any event the moutainous terrain and hot summer temperatures do not lend themseves to cycling. Easier to find for hire are scooters and mopeds. Bikes can be hired more easily, however, on the islands off Sicily which are generally flatter.

Books

Here are a few suggested titles for your holiday reading:

David Gilmour *The Last Leopard: A Life of Giuseppe di Lampedusa*

Giuseppe di Lampedusa *The Leopard*

D H Lawrence *Sicilian Carousel*

Luigi Pirandello *Six Characters in Search of an Author*

Mary Renault *The Mask of Apollo*

Leonardo Sciascia *La Sicilia Come Metafora*

Breakdowns see Accidents

Camping

Camping is popular on Sicily. The sites – the vast majority being on or near the coast – range from the simple to the very sophisticated (1- to 4-star), and prices vary accordingly. At peak times many sites will be full. For full details of all the sites on the island, and booking forms, apply to the Italian Camping Federation (Federcampeggio), Castella Postale 23, 50041 Calenzano, Firenze ☎ **(055) 88 2391**. Otherwise, ask for information from the Italian Tourist Office in your own country (*see* **Tourist Information Offices**). Camping rough is not recommended and is illegal in the national parks.

Car Hire

The main towns and resorts are well stocked with both international and local car-hire agencies, and airlines and tour operators offer fly-drive arrangements; car hire in conjunction with train travel is also available through some of the major car-hire companies.

Weekly rates with unlimited mileage offer the best deal; these include breakdown service and basic insurance but you are advised to take out a collision damage waiver and personal accident insurance.

The small local firms generally offer the cheapest rates, but they can be booked only locally. Most hire companies restrict hire of cars to drivers over 21 (some stipulate a minimum age of 23).

Drivers must have held their full licence for at least a year. With the exception of Avis, there is an upper age limit of 60–65. Unless paying by credit card, a substantial cash deposit is required. Full details of the different hire schemes can be obtained from tourist offices. *See also* **Driving**, **Accidents and Breakdowns** and **Tourist Information Offices**

Churches see Religion

Climate see p.94

Clothing

Spring and autumn are warm and pleasant times of the year to visit Sicily, and during those months light clothes can be worn in the day, with an extra sweater or jacket for the evenings and cooler days. The summer months are very hot indeed; winter, by contrast, can be very cold, particularly in the mountainous areas.

Casual wear is generally acceptable, although smart clothing will be expected for luxurious hotels, restaurants and clubs, and Sicilians generally like to dress up for dinner.

Remember that bare legs and arms are not acceptable (they may even be forbidden) when visiting churches.

Most Italian clothing measurements are standard throughout Europe but differ from those in the UK and the US. The following are examples:

Women's sizes

UK	8	10	12	14	16	18
Italy	38	40	42	44	46	48
US	6	8	10	12	14	16

Men's suits

UK/US	36	38	40	42	44	46
Italy	46	48	50	52	54	56

Men's shirts

UK/US	14	14.5	15	15.5	16	16.5	17
Italy	36	37	38	39/40	41	42	43

Men's shoes

UK	7	7.5	8.5	9.5	10.5	11
Italy	41	42	43	44	45	46
US	8	8.5	9.5	10.5	11.5	12

Women's shoes

UK	4.5	5	5.5	6	6.5	7
Italy	38	38	39	39	40	41
US	6	6.5	7	7.5	8	8.5

Consulates

Australia
Via Alessandria, 215, Rome
☎ (06) 832 721
Canada
Via Zara, 30, Rome
☎ (06) 440 3028
Ireland
Largo del Nazareno 3, Rome
☎ (06) 678 2541
UK
Via Francesco Crispi, 122, Naples ☎ (081) 663 511

Donkey and dog.

USA
Via G B Vaccarini 1, Palermo
☎ **(091) 343 532**

Crime

There is no need to be unduly
concerned about serious crime
in Sicily but it is advisable to
take sensible precautions and
be on your guard at all times.
The main hazards are theft
from cars and snatching
valuables from moving cars – at
traffic lights, for example. Also,
you should be aware that drugs
are widely sold on the street;
do not even be tempted.
• Carry as little money and as
few credit cards as possible,
and leave any valuables in the
hotel safe.
• Carry wallets and purses in
secure pockets inside your
outer clothing, wear body
belts, and carry handbags
across your body or firmly
under your arm.
• Cars, particularly hire cars,
should never be left unlocked,
and you should remove items
of value, including the radio.
• If your passport is lost or
stolen, report it to your
Consulate or Embassy at once.

Currency see Money

Customs and Entry Regulations

There is no limit on the impor-
tation into Sicily of tax-paid
goods bought in an EU
country, provided they are for
personal consumption, with
the exception of alcohol and
tobacco which have fixed limits
governing them.

Disabled Visitors

The *Michelin Red Guide Italia*
indicates which hotels have
facilities for the disabled.

In Britain, RADAR, at 12 City
Forum, 250 City Road, London
EC1V 8AF ☎ **(020) 7250 3222**,
publishes factsheets as well as
an annual guide to facilities
and accommodation overseas,
including Italy.

Italian National Tourist
Offices should also be able to
give information about hotels,
museums, etc. with facilities
(*see* **Tourist Information
Offices**).

Driving

Remember to drive on the
RIGHT, and to give way to
traffic coming from the right –
although you may notice that
some drivers take no notice of
this rule.

Street parking is difficult in
the main towns and it is best to
stick to guarded car parks.
Rimozione forzata indicates that
your car will be towed away.
Never leave valuables,
including radios, in the car as

theft is common.

All of the main routes into towns and cities have petrol stations, and they are found at frequent intervals along motorways. They are normally open 7.30am–noon, and 3–7pm, but opening hours vary, and depend on the season. Unleaded petrol is sold. Very few petrol stations off the motorways accept credit cards. In the interior, petrol stations are few and far between.

There are both toll motorways and non-toll motorways (*autostrade*), all well-surfaced and fast, in Sicily. The main non-motorway roads are the *Strada Statale*. Other Sicilian roads are very variable in quality, and signposting may be non-existent.

The following speed limits apply:

Cars and Motorcycles
Motorways 130kph/80mph (over 1 100cc); 110kph/68mph (under 1 100cc)
Country roads 90kph/56mph
Built-up areas 50kph/31mph
Campers
Motorways 100kph/62mph
Country roads 80kph/50mph
Built-up areas 50kph/31mph

Drivers should carry a full national or international driving licence, and an Italian translation of the licence unless it is a pink European licence. Also take insurance documents including a green card (no longer compulsory for EU members but strongly recommended), registration papers for the car and a nationality sticker for the rear of the car.

Headlight beams should be adjusted for right-hand drive, and a red warning triangle must be carried unless there are hazard warning lights on the car. You should also have a spare set of light bulbs.

The wearing of seatbelts is compulsory (although few Sicilians do); children between nine months and four years must be seated in the back, and babies up to nine months must occupy a baby seat. *See also* **Accidents and Breakdowns**

Electric Current
The voltage in Sicily is usually 220V. Plugs and sockets are of the round, two-pinned variety and adaptors are generally required.

Embassies see Consulates

Emergencies
Ambulance or Police (*Carabinieri*) ☎ 112/113
Fire Service (*Vigili deli Fuoco*) ☎ 115

Colourful fruit stall.

Etiquette

As in most places in the world, when visiting churches and museums visitors are expected to dress discreetly, covering upper legs and arms. Sicilians are courteous people and, although less formal than many other Europeans, greet each other with good morning – *buon giorno*, or good evening – *buona sera*. This is usual when entering a shop, for example.

Women travelling alone should be prepared for a certain amount of unwelcome attention, particularly away from the resorts; consider how you dress, avoid city centres at night and never consider hitching alone.

Guidebooks see Maps

Health

UK nationals should carry a Form E111 (forms are available from post offices in Britain) which is produced by the Department of Health, and which entitles the holder to free urgent treatment for accident or illness in EU countries. The treatment will have to be paid for in the first instance but the cost can be reclaimed later. All foreign nationals are advised to take out comprehensive insurance cover and to keep any bills, receipts and invoices to support any claim.

Lists of doctors can be obtained from hotels, chemists (*farmacia*) or police stations; first aid and medical advice is also available at pharmacies.

First aid (*pronto soccorso*) with

a doctor is also available at airports and railway stations.

Beware of the intense heat in July and August, and of mosquitoes.

Hours *see* **Opening Hours**

Information *see* **Tourist Information Offices**

Language
Sicilians are proud of their knowledge of English but those speaking it are confined to the tourist resorts.

Any effort to speak Italian will be much appreciated everywhere, and even a few simple words and expressions are often warmly received. Below are a few words and phrases to help you make the most of your stay.

Maps
A full range of maps and guides is published by Michelin. These include the Motoring Atlas Italy, which is useful for route-planning if driving to Sicily. Sheet **Map 988** Italy (1/1 000 000) also covers the whole of Italy, and includes Sicily. Sheet **Map 432** Sicily (1/400 000) is ideal for touring the island and has useful street plans of some of the main towns. The *Michelin Green Guide Sicily* contains detailed information on the towns and attractions in Sicily, together with town maps and useful background information to help you get the most from your stay.

Medical Care *see* **Health**

Good morning / Buon giorno
Good afternoon/evening / Buona sera
Yes/no / Si/no
Please/thank you / Per favore/grazie
Do you speak English? / Parla inglese?
How much is it? / Quanto costa questo?
The bill, please / Conto, per favore
Excuse me / Mi scusi
I'd like a stamp / Desidero un francobollo
Do you accept travellers' cheques? / Accetta travellers' cheques?
I don't understand / Non capisco

Money

The monetary unit of Italy is the Italian lira, and notes are issued in denominations of 1 000, 2 000, 5 000, 10 000, 20 000, 50 000 and 100 000 lire. Coins are of 50, 100, 200 and 500 lire. All major credit cards, (American Express, Carte Bleue (Visa/Barclaycard), Diners Club and Eurocard (Mastercard/Access), travellers' cheques and Eurocheques are accepted in most shops, restaurants, hotels, and at some large motorway petrol stations.

There are no restrictions on the amount of currency visitors can take into Sicily; perhaps the safest way to carry large amounts of money is in travellers' cheques which are widely accepted. Bureaux de change are found at airports, larger railway stations and banks (*see also* **Banks**).

Exchange rates vary, so it pays to shop around. You are advised not to pay hotel bills in foreign currency or with travellers' cheques since the hotel's exchange rate is likely to be higher than that of the bureaux de change.

Newspapers

Foreign newspapers and magazines can be bought in the main towns at newsagents

Mosaic of bikini-clad girls, Roman Villa of Casale, Piazza Armerina.

and kiosks, usually one day after publication.

The local daily papers are useful for tourists as they include easily understood sections giving transport timetables, together with other practical information about opening times.

Also useful is the Sicilian *Yellow Pages* for tourists (*Sicilia Pagine Gialle Turismo*), available from the larger tourist offices. It has a multi-language index and listings ranging from accommodation to sports facilities.

Opening Hours

Shops are open 8.30/9am–1pm and 3.30/4pm–7.30/8pm Monday to Saturday. Some may remain open on Sunday in tourist areas.

Chemists are generally open

9am–7.30pm, Monday to Saturday, with some variations. Lists of chemists which are open late or on Sunday are displayed in every pharmacy.

Museums and galleries are usually closed on Sunday afternoon and all day Monday. They are usually open 9am–noon/1pm and sometimes 5–8pm. The siesta is firmly observed; everything will be closed from around noon until 3pm. It should be noted that Sicily carries to an extreme form the leisurely Italian approach to restoration. Some museums and churches are closed for years on end.

Churches The main churches are open all day but others close in the afternoon 1pm–3pm; many stay closed after 3pm.

Photography

Good-quality film and camera equipment are readily available, but expensive, in Sicily generally. Before taking photographs in museums and art galleries you should check with staff, as photography is sometimes restricted. Generally it is permitted in state-owned museums, although the use of flash and tripods is not, but you need special permission to film in municipal museums. Never leave cameras in cars.

Police

The *carabinieri* deal with serious crime; the *polizia di stato* handle general crime, including lost passports and theft reports for insurance claims; the *polizia stradale* handle traffic control outside

Scooters and motorbikes, Cefalù.

towns; and the *vigili urbani* deal with town traffic and administration. Police stations (*questura*) can be found in the main towns.

Post Offices
Post offices are usually open 8am–1/1.30pm, Monday to Friday, 9am–noon on Saturday; main post offices in larger towns remain open all day, sometimes until 7pm. In Palermo, the main post office, in Via Roma, is open 24 hours.

Stamps (*francobolli*) are sold in post offices and tobacconists (*tabacchi*), which display a black sign with a white 'T', and in some bars. The postal service is not particularly speedy: urgent letters should be sent *espresso*.

Telegrams can be sent from post offices, SIP telephone offices or by dialling ☎ **186** from a private phone.

Public Holidays
New Year's Day: 1 January
Epiphany: 6 January
Easter Day and Easter Monday
Liberation Day: 25 April
Labour Day: 1 May
Assumption Day: 15 August
All Saints' Day: 1 November
Immaculate Conception:
    8 December
Christmas Day: 25 December
Boxing Day: 26 December

Public Transport
see **Transport**

Religion
Italy is a Roman Catholic country and mass is celebrated in Italian in most churches in Sicily every Sunday. For details of services in other languages, or of churches of other denominations, contact the local tourist board or ask at your hotel.

Smoking
Smoking is banned in churches, museums and art galleries but elsewhere is widely accepted. There are separate non-smoking compartments in trains.

Tobacconists (*tabacchi*) sell the major international brands of cigarettes, which are also on sale in bars and restaurants.

Stamps see **Post Offices**

Taxis see **Transport**

Telephones
Kiosks take telephone cards (*schede telefoniche*) to the value of 5 000, 10 000 and 15 000 lire, sold at newsagents and tobacconists, or 100, 200 and 500 lire coins, or tokens (*gettoni*). You can dial anywhere in Italy and abroad from these telephone boxes.

Calls can also made from offices of SIP, the telephone company, in Palermo and Catania and the airports. Here the call is metered and you pay afterwards.

As in most countries, telephone calls made from hotels may be more straightforward and convenient, but they are more expensive.

Cheap rates apply 10pm–8am, Monday to Saturday, and all day Sunday. For information, ☎ 12. Country codes are as follows:
Australia: ☎ 00 61
Canada: ☎ 00 1
Ireland: ☎ 00 353
New Zealand: ☎ 00 64
UK: ☎ 00 44
USA: ☎ 00 1

To call Italy from abroad, ☎ 00 39, and for Palermo add 091.

Time Difference

Italian standard time is one hour ahead of GMT. Italian Summer Time (IST) begins on the last weekend in March when the clocks go forward an hour (the same day as British Summer Time), and ends on the last weekend in September when the clocks go back (one month before BST ends).

Tipping

A service charge of 10 or 15 per cent is usually included in the bill at hotels and restaurants in Italy but a tip (minimum amount 1 000 lire) can also be given where the service has been particularly pleasing.

Usherettes who show you to your seat in a cinema or theatre should receive a small amount, as should hotel, airport and railway porters, and lavatory attendants. Taxi drivers will expect about 10 per cent.

Tourist Information Offices

The Italian State Tourist Office (ENIT) is a good initial source of information about Sicily, including accommodation, travel and places of interest.

It has offices in the following English-speaking countries:
Australia and New Zealand ENIT, c/o Alitalia, Orient Overseas Building, Suite 202, 32 Bridge Street, Sydney, NSW 2000 ☎ 2 92 471 308
Canada 1 Place Ville-Marie, Suite 1914, Montreal, Quebec, H3B 3M9 ☎ (514) 866 7667
UK 1 Princes Street, London W1R 8AY ☎ (020) 7408 1254
US 630 Fifth Avenue, Suite 1565, New York, NY 10111 ☎ (212) 245 4822

Italy is divided into 20 regions, of which Sicily counts as one, each with a Regional

Tourist Board. The regions are further divided into provinces which each have a provincial capital; these in turn each have a tourist board, officially called AAPIT (Azienda Autonoma Provinciale per l'Incremento Turistico) but also still known as EPT (Ente Provinciale Turismo) or APT (Azienda Promozione Turistica). These tourist boards run information offices (where foreign languages, including English, are spoken) throughout their province; they publish numerous brochures and leaflets and provide information about all aspects of the area.

Palmero: Piazza Castelnuovo 34 ☎ 091 583 847

Catania: Via Cimarosa 10 ☎ 095 73 06 211

Tours

Practically all travel agents in the major resorts offer a number of organised tours. Most of the major hotels also offer coach tours to highlights of the area.

Transport

If you intend to stay at more than one place or really want to explore the island, a car is probably the best option although public transport is reasonable, if sometimes rather erratic and slow.
See **Car Hire** and **Newspapers**.

Air: As well as the international airports, there are small airports at Trapini Birgi, Lampedusa and Pantelleria dealing with internal flights.

Train: Italy's national railway (FS), connecting the major towns, is reasonably efficient and relatively inexpensive in Sicily. Tickets can be purchased at stations and at many travel agents. Categories of trains are as follows: *locale* – very slow, stops often; *diritto* – fewer stops; *expresso* – stops at main towns only; Intercity trains – connect big cities only; Eurocity trains – link major

Relaxing in Cefalù.

European cities. Various passes and discounts are available which can be arranged in advance at a CIT.

Bus: There is a fairly extensive network of regional buses in Sicily (*autobus* or *pullman*). They are usually quicker and more reliable than the train but more expensive (with the exception of the Palermo to Messina route). Two main companies, SAIS and AST, cover most of the island. Departure is usually from the railway station, if there is one. Tickets must be purchased in advance.

In cities, the city buses are the quickest and easiest way of getting around. Tickets must be bought before boarding from a bus company office or a *tabacchi* and then validated on boarding the bus.

Boat: Ferries and hydrofoils run regularly to Sicily's islands. During the summer they operate frequently but during the winter may dwindle to two or three a week. Prices on the whole tend to be low.

Taxis: These can generally be found in special taxi ranks at railway stations and in the main squares of towns; they can also be called by telephone or hailed in the street. Fares are displayed on the meters; there are extra charges at night, on Sunday and public holidays, for luggage and for journeys outside the town, e.g. to airports.

TV and Radio

There are three state-run television channels, RAI 1, 2 and 3, mostly offering a popular mix of American and Brazilian soaps and sitcoms and Italian cabaret shows. Note that the private companies sometimes show pornographic films during the day.

Radio is not much more adventurous, with numerous very local stations featuring chat and pop music. The RAI stations do include news and current affairs.

Vaccinations
see **Before You Go p.112**

Youth Hostels
see **Accommodation**

Water

Generally, tap water is safe to drink although supplies marked *'Non potabile'* should not be used for drinking. Drinking water from village pumps is not advised and during the summer months supplies may be restricted in some areas.

INDEX

INDEX